The Battle of Cedar Creek

THE BATTLE OF CEDAR CREEK

VICTORY FROM THE JAWS OF DEFEAT

JONATHAN A. NOYALAS

SERIES EDITOR DOUGLAS W. BOSTICK

Charleston London
THE History PRESS

Published by The History Press
Charleston, SC 29403
www.historypress.net

First published 2009
Second printing 2011
Third printing 2012
Fourth printing 2012

Manufactured in the United States
ISBN 978.1.59629.593.3

Library of Congress Cataloging-in-Publication Data
Noyalas, Jonathan A.
The Battle of Cedar Creek : victory from the jaws of defeat / Jonathan A. Noyalas.
p. cm.
Includes bibliographical references.
ISBN 978-1-59629-593-3
1. Cedar Creek, Battle of, Va., 1864. I. Title.
E477.33.N69 2009
973.7'37--dc22
2009039317

Dedicated with love to my son, Alexander Philip, with whom
I look forward to exploring Civil War battlefields.

Contents

Preface

With the approaching Civil War sesquicentennial our American Republic has the great opportunity to reflect, learn and, when necessary, reinterpret the American Civil War to help gain a clearer understanding of how those four years of bloody conflict defined this nation. Since the Civil War's end, veterans of the conflict and, later, historians chronicled the events of that struggle, and with each passing generation the Civil War's story has been retold. Tens of thousands of books about battles, campaigns and generals have been produced since the cessation of hostilities in 1865. The large outpouring of published material has seemed to convince some that nothing else could be written about the Civil War; however, interpretation of the past is not stagnant, nor should it ever become so. New evidence and fresh perspectives prompt each generation of historians to reexamine the Civil War's key moments and redefine how the Civil War is viewed and taught. This book continues in that tradition.

From regimental historians of the immediate postwar years to more modern authors such as Thomas Lewis, Theodore Mahr, Joseph Whitehorne and Jeffry Wert, the Battle of Cedar Creek has proven a topic worthy of discussion, as the battle yielded significant military and political results. This volume—intended to bring the Battle of Cedar Creek to life in a more succinct fashion for individuals with varying interests in our nation's epic struggle—builds upon new research and attempts to offer some new insights into the Shenandoah Valley's greatest battle: namely, that the battle impacted civilians of the Middletown area, whose peaceful existence was interrupted by the armies of General Philip H. Sheridan and General Jubal A. Early; that the fighting of the Nineteenth Corps during the battle's morning phase played a vital role in the success of the Army of the Shenandoah and has been underappreciated; an examination of how Cedar Creek defined Sheridan's legacy; and that the monuments erected on the battlefield and postwar reunions held on that hallowed ground served a crucial role in postwar reconciliation in the Shenandoah Valley.

In constructing this volume I have relied heavily upon the primary accounts left by participants, some of which are in private collections and appear in this volume for the first time. Additionally, newspaper accounts, postwar reunion speeches and other primary materials were utilized to reconstruct the battle's story and legacy.

Writing this book has been a tremendous undertaking and would not have been possible without the help of countless individuals. The people I recognize have in some way contributed to this project, but are in no way at fault for any of its errors: the staff of the Beinecke Rare Book and Manuscripts Library at Yale University who made the Thomas Buchanan Read Papers available; Nan Card at the Rutherford B. Hayes Presidential Center in Fremont, Ohio, who has always been gracious in supporting my research on the Valley; Suzanne Chilson and the Cedar Creek Battlefield Foundation, who let me cull through their files; my dear friend and colleague Dr. Geraldine Keifer, associate professor of art history at Shenandoah University, who has been a great collaborator in researching the impact of Sheridan's Ride; the staff of the Macculloch Hall Historical Museum in Morristown, New Jersey; Mr. Blake Magner, who prepared the battle maps; Mr. Fred Molineux of Pittstown, New Jersey; the staff at the Museum of the Confederacy in Richmond, Virginia; my dear friend Nicholas Picerno, who opened up his collections and who has been a constant supporter of my work and research; my friend and fellow board member of the Kernstown Battlefield Association, Scott Patchan, who provided an obscure newspaper reference to Sheridan's Ride; the staff of the Stewart Bell Jr. Archives in the Handley Regional Library in Winchester, Virginia, especially archivist Rebecca Ebert and Jerry Holsworth, who assisted me in my research at that superb institution; the staff of the United States Army Military History Institute in Carlisle, Pennsylvania; Dr. Joseph Whitehorne, my friend and colleague at Lord Fairfax Community College and Cedar Creek expert who always answered any questions I had pertaining to the battle and guided me to some important research material; and Karen Wisecarver, the interlibrary loan specialist at my institution, Lord Fairfax Community College, who went above and beyond the call of duty. Last, but certainly not least, I would like to thank the love of my life, my wife, Brandy, a fine historian and teacher, whose research assistance and advice has been invaluable.

Introduction

Several decades after the Civil War, veterans of the 128th New York gathered on the Cedar Creek battlefield to dedicate their regimental monument. During the dedication, one veteran stated of Cedar Creek's importance, "I do not believe there is a spot on this continent, where more for the interests of our nation was concentrated than here at Cedar Creek."[1] While some might believe that this New Yorker exaggerated the battle's importance (not uncommon in postwar dedications), one could sternly argue that because of what was at stake for the Union in the autumn of 1864, Cedar Creek, if only for a moment, indeed became one of the most important places in North America.

Among all of the battles fought in the Shenandoah Valley, none achieved more significant results and had wider consequences than Cedar Creek. Militarily, the battle finally wrested the Shenandoah Valley—the Confederacy's breadbasket—from Confederate grip and prevented the Valley's harvests from being utilized by Confederate forces operating in the Old Dominion. Politically, the Union victory at Cedar Creek tremendously aided President Abraham Lincoln's bid for reelection in November 1864. Additionally, Cedar Creek also defined the military legacy of General Philip H. Sheridan and elevated him to the great pantheon of American generals. This battle more than any other of his life made him an American hero, at least in the popular American consciousness. Beyond the impact the battle had on wartime strategy and the lives of both Lincoln and Sheridan, it played a significant role in defining the military service of the enlisted men who fought under Sheridan during the 1864 Shenandoah Campaign. During the postwar era of reconciliation, which began in the early 1880s, Cedar Creek's hallowed ground provided an ideal setting for both veterans of Blue and Gray to gather and honor the gallantry of the American citizen soldier while simultaneously helping to heal the nation's wounds.

Cedar Creek's story is compelling and important not only to Civil War history, but also to national history. The battle, the field, the men who fought there and the veterans who returned to remember and reconcile all represent the sacrifice of war, as well as hope for future healing among former enemies.

Chapter 1

No Longer "the Valley of humiliation"

Nestled between the Allegheny Mountains on the west and the Blue Ridge on the east, Virginia's Shenandoah Valley enjoyed tremendous economic prosperity in the decades prior to the Civil War. The fertile land produced abundant crops of wheat and corn, while key towns such as Staunton, Winchester and Harpers Ferry enjoyed additional financial success as transportation hubs.[2] Ironically, this economic prosperity that made the Shenandoah Valley thrive also made it the target of both armies during our American Iliad and brought about its demise.

The Shenandoah Valley owed its wartime strategic significance to a number of factors. First, the Valley supplied numerous resources to the Confederacy, particularly forces operating in Virginia—the heart of the Confederacy. The materials that Valley farmers supplied to Confederate troops earned the Valley its nickname, the "Breadbasket of the Confederacy." Additionally, the Shenandoah Valley served as an avenue of invasion for Confederate armies into the North and also served as a point from which Confederate forces could threaten Washington, D.C. Due to its geographic location, Confederate war planners also utilized the Valley as a place from which to create a strategic diversion and alleviate pressure against Richmond. Union forces likewise looked to the Valley as a point from which they could protect Washington, D.C., disrupt invasion and diminish the Valley's capacity to supply food and material to the Confederate war effort.[3]

Throughout the conflict's first three years, the Confederacy enjoyed the upper hand in the Valley. After suffering constant defeat, many in the North referred to the Shenandoah Valley as the "Valley of humiliation." A Vermont soldier recalled, "To many a Federal general it had been the valley of humiliation, on account of the defeats his forces had suffered

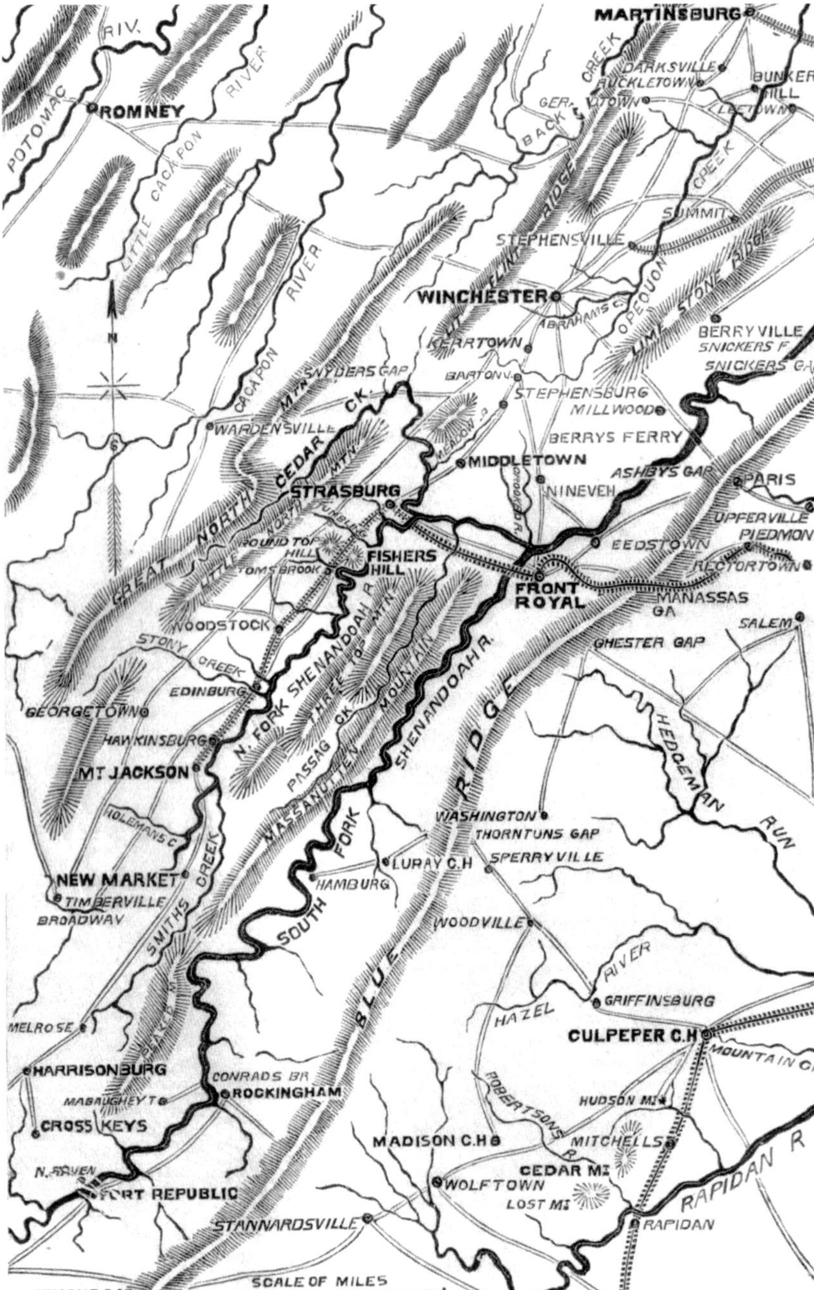

The Shenandoah Valley in 1864. *Pictorial History of the Great Civil War, 1870.*

[none] had been able to destroy the enemy west of the Blue Ridge, or drive the Confederate armies from that land of abundance, where they gathered strength to prolong the conflict, and from which they raided the other side of the Potomac and menaced Washington."[4] Aggravated over the inability of Union forces to secure the Valley, General Ulysses S. Grant aimed to do something about it in the summer of 1864.

Grant fumed with indignation after Confederate forces under General Jubal A. Early threatened Washington, D.C., in early July and defeated the Army of West Virginia at the Second Battle of Kernstown on July 24, and Confederate cavalry under General John McCausland raided and burned Chambersburg several days later. Grant knew that as long as Confederate forces succeeded in the Valley, his operations to hammer General Robert E. Lee's Army of Northern Virginia into submission around Petersburg and subsequently capture Richmond would suffer. Incensed over the use of the Valley as a diversionary theater and avenue of invasion, Grant decided to consolidate the Department of the Susquehanna, Middle Department, Department of Washington and Department of the West into the Middle Military Division. Grant, the general-in-chief of the Union army, fully understood that at no point in the war did the various armies operating in the region attempt to cooperate with one another. In addition to a lack of military cohesion among the various Union commands in the area, Grant further recognized the War Department's inability to comprehend the true strategic nature of the Valley. It appeared to Grant that war planners in Washington used the Valley merely as a buffer for the capital. "It seemed to be the policy of General Halleck and Secretary Stanton, to keep any force sent there," Grant observed, "in pursuit of the invading army, moving right and left so as to keep between the enemy and our capital; and, generally speaking they pursued this policy until all knowledge of the whereabouts of the enemy was lost."[5]

General Ulysses S. Grant fought tenaciously for Sheridan's appointment to command. *Author's collection.*

Following his decision to create the Middle Military Division, Grant realized that this new force needed an aggressive commander to take charge of the approximately forty thousand soldiers in its ranks who could then finally wrest the Valley from Confederate hands. He initially suggested Major General William B. Franklin, a former classmate and friend from West Point, to President Abraham Lincoln and Secretary of War Edwin Stanton. Lincoln vehemently disapproved of Grant's first choice. A Democrat, Franklin constantly criticized the Lincoln administration and had supported former Union General George B. McClellan for the presidency in 1864. Additionally, Franklin's reputation had been tarnished by his seeming lack of aggressiveness as commander of the Left Grand Division at the Battle of Fredericksburg in December 1862.[6] Lincoln understood that the outcome of the campaign in the Valley would contribute to his success or failure at the polls in November, and he dared not put his political fate in the hands of a known detractor.

After Franklin, Grant suggested Major General George G. Meade, the current commander of the Army of the Potomac. Lincoln also disliked this idea. The president reminded Grant that a number of individuals had pressured him to remove Meade from command. With the election only months away, Lincoln did not want to appear as if he had caved into the wishes of a few individuals.[7] Finally Grant suggested Major General Philip H. Sheridan. Initially Lincoln appeared comfortable with the decision, but Stanton did not. Although Sheridan was a West Point graduate and had performed well with Grant in the west and as a cavalry commander in the Army of the Potomac, Stanton believed that Sheridan was too young for such an important post, particularly months away from Lincoln's reelection bid. "Mr. Stanton objected," Grant recalled, "on the ground that he was too young for so important a command."[8] Grant, however, had endless faith in Sheridan's abilities to be aggressive in the Valley. The general-in-chief believed that Sheridan had "no superior as a general, either living or dead, and perhaps not an equal."[9] Once Grant calmed Stanton's fears, Sheridan met with approval and received the promotion to command of the newly minted Middle Military Division—soon to become popularly known as the Army of the Shenandoah.

Sheridan's appointment formally came on August 6, 1864, and met with mixed reaction among the troops charged with doing what no other Union general had been able to do before—removing the Confederacy's firm grip on the Shenandoah Valley. Three days after Sheridan's appointment, Colonel Charles Russell Lowell wrote his wife from Harpers Ferry—the launching

General Philip H. Sheridan. *Author's collection.*

point for Sheridan's 1864 Shenandoah Campaign—"Everything is in chaos here, but under Sheridan is rapidly assuming shape. It was a lucky inspiration of Grant's or Lincoln's to make a Middle Military Division and put him in command of it."[10] Some of Sheridan's men seemed inspired by his mere presence and manner of confidence. General Emory Upton explained to his sister that "General Sheridan has the appearance of great nerve, and hitherto has been quite successful. For one, I am better pleased with his appearance than that of any other commander under whom I have served."[11]

Still, not all troops were sold on Sheridan. A New Yorker recalled, "Gen. Sheridan was a man, but little known at this time, and many were the expressions of surprise that an officer of so little distinction should be placed in charge of such an immense command."[12] Other troops in the Army of the Shenandoah who knew little about Sheridan decided to put their trust in Grant's judgment. "Of Gen'l. Sheridan we knew very little. His name had been associated with some brilliant cavalry exploits," recalled a veteran of the 116th New York, "but much regret was manifested that some man better known…had not been selected. Gen'l. Grant, however, knew better than we the duties to be performed."[13] While many passed judgment on Sheridan, some, such as the Twenty-ninth Maine's William Knowlton, decided to wait and see what Sheridan would do during the campaign in the Valley. "General Sheridan has assumed the command of this Department and he has now a very strong force…what he will do remains to be seen," Knowlton explained to his wife on August 9.[14]

Throughout August and the first half of September, Sheridan organized his command—the Sixth Corps under General Horatio Wright, the Eighth Corps (Army of West Virginia) under General George Crook, the Nineteenth

Corps under General William Emory and his cavalry corps under General Alfred T.A. Torbert. Sheridan's first month of command witnessed some skirmishes and a lot of maneuvering, but no major battles. While some became incensed over Sheridan's apparent lack of aggressiveness, he had been instructed by Grant to be pragmatic and know precisely the whereabouts and strength of Early's army before he attacked. Sheridan fully understood the implications of a premature offensive and subsequent Union defeat in the Valley. "I knew that I was strong, yet, in consequence of the injunctions of General Grant, I deemed it necessary to be very cautious," Sheridan explained, "and the fact that the Presidential election was impending made me doubly so, the authorities at Washington having impressed upon me that the defeat of my army might be followed by the overthrow of the party in power."[15] The lack of activity frustrated and confused some of Sheridan's soldiers, but others understood that the new commander had sound reasons for his pragmatism. "It was Sheridan's first independent command," wrote a soldier in the 121st New York, "and he was cautioned against attempting any general engagement until his army had become unified in operation, and more developed in morale."[16]

Finally, on September 19, 1864, Sheridan launched his campaign with a victory at the Third Battle of Winchester.[17] Three days later the Army of the Shenandoah followed up its successes with victory at the Battle of Fisher's Hill. Following those two victories in three days, Sheridan then set to the work of destroying the Shenandoah Valley as the "Breadbasket of the Confederacy." Over a period of thirteen days Sheridan's command embarked upon its campaign of destruction known as "the Burning" where grain, livestock, barns and mills were destroyed to prevent their use by the Confederate war effort. Sheridan's troops reportedly destroyed approximately 1,200 barns and over 435,000 bushels of wheat, and they seized approximately 11,000 heads of cattle.[18] This act of widespread destruction earned Sheridan the eternal enmity of many Valley residents. John O. Casler, a resident of the lower Valley who served in the Thirty-third Virginia Infantry as part of Early's Valley army in 1864, condemned Sheridan's campaign of destruction. "Poverty stared the citizens in the face, as this was in the fall season of the year," Casler observed, "and too late to raise any provisions. Their horses and cattle were all gone, their farm implements burnt and no prospects of producing anything the next year."[19] John Opie, a Confederate cavalryman who served in the Valley, noted that Sheridan's troops had destroyed "all food for man, or beast, that could be found…Horses, cattle, cows, sheep, hogs and poultry were either killed and fed to the army, or shot down and left in the fields."[20]

Although Confederate sympathizers viewed Sheridan's campaign as brutal, some Union troops regarded it as a military necessity in order to bring about the war's end. "A large portion of the supplies for the rebel army at Richmond were drawn from this exceedingly rich section of the country," explained a member of the 116th New York. "It supplied Early entirely thus making his occupation of it an easy matter. Had this sharply been sooner cut off, it would have been impossible for him to have constantly threatened Maryland and Pennsylvania with invasion. War is terrible, and this was but one of the evils which the chivalry should have expected."[21]

In addition to the Burning, Sheridan's cavalry struck another blow to Confederate morale and strength in the Valley with a victory over Confederate cavalry under General Thomas Rosser at the Battle of Tom's Brook on October 9. The Army of the Shenandoah's successes raised spirits in the North. The *New York Tribune*, for example, reported that Sheridan's success at the Third Battle of Winchester "flashes upon us as the First Victory in that Valley of the Shenandoah which hitherto has been to us a Valley of Humiliation and almost Despair."[22]

Confidence among the Army of the Shenandoah soared in the aftermath of the Union cavalry's success at Tom's Brook. Some Union soldiers believed that Tom's Brook signaled the end of Sheridan's Campaign. "Our campaign in the Valley is supposed to be ended. It winds up with a most signal cavalry victory," Colonel Rutherford B. Hayes wrote to his wife following the battle.[23] Following the cavalry's triumph, Sheridan pulled his command north from Strasburg to a defensive position along the north bank of Cedar Creek, south of Middletown, on October 10. "General Sheridan, having burned all the grain and forage in the Upper Shenandoah, had leisurely fallen back far enough to keep his communications safe," recalled a veteran of the 114th New York, "and was establishing a line of defense which should hold the richest and most fertile part of the Valley."[24] In addition to the natural defense of Cedar Creek, the Shenandoah River on the army's eastern flank, along with the base of Massanutten Mountain, Sheridan's command entrenched and established a defensive position that had the initial perception of being strong.[25] "Elaborate earthworks were planned, and with much labor constructed," recalled a soldier in the 116th New York, "so that the position was considered almost impregnable."[26] Although the task of digging the earthworks proved hard work, a sizable portion of the troops in Sheridan's command welcomed the monotonous labor. One soldier recalled simply that it provided a "respite from fatiguing marches and terrible battles."[27]

The apparent strength of the Union position—coupled with the confidence among Sheridan's troops that Early had been whipped and no longer remained a threat in the Valley—caused the Army of the Shenandoah's optimism to soar by the second week of October.[28] Some troops even believed that by October 15 the Army of the Shenandoah would be sent from the Valley to Washington, D.C. Other troops believed that Early's Confederates had departed the Valley completely and that the Army of the Shenandoah would be pulled back to Winchester to establish winter camps. Major George Nye of the Twenty-ninth Maine wrote on October 13, "I hardly think the Rebs will visit the Valley again in a hurry…it is rumored that we are going back to Winchester."[29] Rumors circulated furiously throughout Sheridan's army; however, circumstances would prove that the optimism many Union soldiers shared was premature, as Early was not yet willing to declare defeat and turn the Confederacy's Breadbasket over to Sheridan's army.

CHAPTER 2

"A MORE PERFECT FEELING OF SECURITY"

As confidence among Sheridan's army soared, General Early contemplated the next move for his command. On October 9, Early penned a message to General Robert E. Lee and informed him that he was "satisfied that he [Sheridan] does not intend coming this way again, as he burnt all the bridges in his rear as he went down." While Early felt confident that Sheridan would not march south, he expressed uncertainty as to what Sheridan intended to do next. "Whether he will move across the Ridge," Early pondered, "send a part of his force to Grant, or content himself with protecting the Baltimore and Ohio." Old Jube did not know. General Early understood his strategic mission of diversion in the Valley—to hold as many Union troops as possible in the Shenandoah and away from Grant's lines around Petersburg. Early informed Lee that if Sheridan moved across the Blue Ridge Mountains he would "move directly across from this place to meet him." Although he had already been crushed in battle by Sheridan, Early informed Lee that if Sheridan's men got into the Blue Ridge Mountains his Confederate forces could "defeat [Sheridan's] infantry and thwart his movements on the east side of the mountains." Another possibility that Early confronted was that Sheridan might send part of his army to Grant and keep another in the lower Valley. Early did not have enough troops to deal with that type of situation. Furthermore, he understood that his army confronted an additional problem—supplies. The Confederate commander in the Valley informed Lee that Sheridan "laid waste nearly all of Rockingham and Shenandoah, and I will have to rely on Augusta for my supplies, and they are not abundant there." Despite the uncertainties and obstacles that confronted Early's army, he noted that his "infantry is now in good heart and condition."[30]

Above, left: General Jubal A. Early. *Battles and Leaders*.

Above, right: General John B. Gordon. *Battles and Leaders*.

Before he obtained any guidance from Lee, Early received some startling news late on October 11—Sheridan had ordered General Horatio Wright's Sixth Corps to move from the Valley to reinforce Grant at Petersburg. At sunrise the following day, Early marched his army north toward Fisher's Hill. By the late morning of October 13, the lead elements of Early's army—General John B. Gordon's division—arrived at Hupp's Hill, just south of Sheridan's camps along Cedar Creek. Soon Confederate artillery rolled into position on Hupp's Hill and opened fire on the Union position.[31] Captain Jedediah Hotchkiss recalled that the gunners opened on Union troops around Belle Grove and "scattered them." A soldier in the Thirty-fourth Massachusetts, whose camp rested on the east side of the Valley Pike and southeast of the Belle Grove mansion, noted that the sound of the artillery startled some of the men in the regiment. "The Rebels were popping away at us," recalled a veteran of the Thirty-fourth, "from a hill on the other side of the creek, and had our range as accurately as if they had been engaged for a long time, instead of but a few minutes."[32] Uncertain of what this artillery bombardment meant, General George Crook, along with General William Emory, decided to send Colonel Joseph Thoburn's division on a reconnaissance to locate the enemy position, determine their strength and find out their intentions.

Thoburn's two brigades—one commanded by Colonel George Wells and another by Colonel Thomas M. Harris—crossed Cedar Creek. As the brigades advanced over the Stickley Farm, the Confederates increased their fire. "The Rebels concentrated their fire upon this ground as we moved over it," recalled a soldier in Wells's brigade, "but the old Regiment had seen too much hot work during the summer to flinch at such a time."[33] Additionally, General James Conner's brigade from General Joseph Kershaw's division moved forward to slow the Union advance. In addition to the two Union brigades, Federal artillery deployed to a high knoll on the west side of the Valley Pike overlooking the Stickley House and opened fire on the Confederates. Captain Hotchkiss recalled only, "We also suffered some from the Yankee artillery."[34] Union artillery support, however, did not offer enough resistance to slow the Confederates adequately. When Thoburn's brigades locked horns with Conner's command, the officers on the field realized that the Confederates had a sizable force and that they should not press their enemy. "The whole line had now become fiercely engaged with the enemy's infantry," recalled Colonel Harris, "and it soon became apparent that he was there in such force as to enable him to turn our right, and that he had already initiated movements to this end." Confronted with a substantial Confederate force whose intentions remained unknown, Thoburn's brigades withdrew in "some disorder."[35]

The fight lasted for approximately one hour and Thoburn's brigades suffered 209 casualties, with nearly 75 percent of them coming from Colonel Wells's brigade.[36] Among the casualties in that brigade was Colonel Wells, who received a mortal wound. During the retreat Wells's men tried desperately to get their brigade commander off the field. Wells urged the men to take care of themselves, but still they tried to save him. As the Union troops attempted to get off the field, several officers from the Thirty-fourth Massachusetts, Wells's original regiment, were greeted by General Jubal Early. Old Jube inquired as to the identity of the brigade commander, and when the men revealed that it was Colonel Wells, Early called for an ambulance. As the men placed Wells into the ambulance he breathed his last. "Thus died our beloved commander; always brave and cool," recalled an officer of the regiment, "strict in discipline, and thoughtful for the welfare of his soldiers, and the reputation of the Regiment."[37]

The following day, the veterans of the Thirty-fourth Massachusetts retrieved Wells's body and sent it to his family in Massachusetts for a proper burial. As Union soldiers brought Wells's body back to Union lines, the men reflected on his greatness and character. "God only knows

Colonel George Wells, mortally wounded on October 13, 1864. *Author's collection.*

how tenderly and sincerely we all loved him," recalled the Thirty-fourth Massachusetts's Captain Charles Elwell, "and how grieved and heart stricken we are at his loss. The 34th has lost its idol; and the service [of] one of the best officers that ever stood before the enemy."[38]

The small fight on October 13 caused Sheridan to realize that Early was not yet ready to capitulate and still determined to remain in the Valley. What Sheridan did not know, however, was the extent to which Early's battered army would show aggression. In any event, Sheridan now had no choice but to recall General Wright's Sixth Corps to the Valley. "The day's events pointing to a probability that the enemy intended to resume the offensive," Sheridan explained, "to anticipate such a contingency I ordered the Sixth Corps to return from its march."[39] For the moment, Early had been able to prolong his mission of strategic diversion, but he knew that Sheridan's army was still too large and in too strong of a position to be assaulted without proper planning. Without sufficient strength and lack of a plan for the moment Early pulled back to Fisher's Hill "and waited to see whether the enemy would move."[40]

As Early's force gathered on Fisher's Hill, confidence among most Union troops continued to soar despite the fight on October 13. Even though both armies rested within only about five miles of each other, the majority of troops in the Army of the Shenandoah still did not regard Early as a real threat. "Although the rebel army, reinforced and resupplied with artillery, had come back to Fisher's Hill…the two bitter antagonists…regarded each other with singular apathy," recalled a soldier in the 114th New York. Colonel Benjamin F. Coates, who commanded a brigade in the Eighth Corps, exemplified the confidence that many in the army felt that second week of October: "I do not think another battle will result, I have no fears of their

[Confederates] attacking us in our general position as they must know that if they do we will whip them as our position is a very good one."[41]

After Sheridan's initial anxieties caused by the fight on October 13, he reevaluated his position and felt confident that Early would not dare launch a major offensive against the numerically superior Union army. Sheridan believed that after Early saw the Army of the Shenandoah still firmly in its position along the northern bank of Cedar Creek, the Confederate forces would remain "at Fisher's Hill and not accomplish much."[42] With renewed optimism, Sheridan made several key decisions. First, Sheridan decided to send elements of his cavalry to Front Royal with the intent of then sending it via Chester Gap to Charlottesville, where it could disrupt the Virginia Central Railroad. Sheridan also agreed to accept Secretary of War Stanton's invitation to come to Washington, D.C., to discuss strategic matters. On the evening of October 15, Sheridan, with plans in place, made his way toward Washington. When he departed the Army of the Shenandoah, Sheridan left General Wright in temporary command. The following day Sheridan received a message from Wright that again prompted Sheridan to alter his plans. Wright informed Sheridan that he had intercepted a message sent from the Confederate signal station at Signal Knob that stated Early's small army would be reinforced by troops from General James Longstreet's command. When Sheridan received this news he initially thought that it "was a ruse" but still he decided to err on the side of caution and ordered the Union cavalry to halt their operations against the Virginia Central Railroad and return to the Army of the Shenandoah at once.[43]

General Horatio Wright, temporary commander of the Army of the Shenandoah. *Author's collection.*

While Sheridan reacted to each piece of news he received after October 15 with great caution and made certain that the Army of the Shenandoah would not be left in a vulnerable situation, Early's troops wondered about future operations in the Valley. Some of Early's men hoped they would remain atop Fisher's Hill and do nothing. Captain D. Augustus Dickert, who served in the Third South Carolina and who had been involved in the fight on the thirteenth, noted that the men of his regiment "expected that we would have a long, sweet rest—a rest so much needed and devoutly wished for, after two months of incessant marching and fighting."[44] While Dickert wanted rest, other Confederate soldiers noted that, although they welcomed a respite from the fighting, they also wanted to eat. Supplies in Early's army were low and the ability to forage almost impossible. "We were surrounded by difficulties," recalled the Thirteenth Virginia's Captain Samuel Buck. "Every mill had been destroyed and no way to get flour or meal and no forage for horses."[45]

Additionally, Early had to consider how the Valley's devastation impacted the soldiers who called the Shenandoah Valley home. Numerous troops in Early's army who had family in the Valley weighed their options as to whether they should remain in the army or go home and care for their families. William Wartmann, a justice in Rockingham County, warned Confederate officials that the dire situation for many families in the Valley might compel men in the ranks of Early's army to desert. Furthermore, Justice Wartmann believed that conditions in the Valley would prompt young men conscripted into the Confederacy's service to resist their enlistment in favor of staying at home to take care of their families. "It will require the daily and hourly exertions of the poor and those who have been burnt out to procure a scanty subsistence to sustain life during the winter. When the soldier now in the army learns that his neighbor," Wartmann advised, "on whom his family has leaned for support, and his family (his wife and little children at home) are to suffer, *he will become uneasy in his* place, and will weigh the duty he owes his family; and what the promptings of nature would be is not difficult to determine."[46] Confronted with these obstacles along with his mission of strategic diversion, Early believed he had no other alternative than to fight. Early observed the Army of the Shenandoah until October 16 and hoped that it would leave its position; however, when it remained Early wanted an accurate assessment of the Union position's true strength. On October 17, Early sent General Gordon with one brigade from his division to Hupp's Hill to reconnoiter the Union position. When Gordon returned he told Early that it was indeed fortified with earthworks. With this news Early weighed the two options that every soldier in his army understood were available to their commander—fight or withdraw. "I was now compelled to move back for want of provisions and forage, or attack the enemy in his position with the hope of driving him from it," Early observed. With his two alternatives clear, Early "determined to attack."[47]

After Early decided to assault the Army of the Shenandoah, the next question he had to answer was how to attack the fortified Union position. A direct frontal assault was out of the question, and so he looked to assess the feasibility of striking either flank of the Union army. On the night of October 17, General Gordon, along with his chief of staff Major Robert W. Hunter, Brigadier General Clement Evans and chief topographical engineer Captain Jedediah Hotchkiss, scaled Massanutten Mountain to observe the Union position. From their perch, the officers agreed that the only place an attack could be made was against the Union left. These Confederate officers were not the only ones to believe that the weakness of the Union line was its eastern flank:[48] Union artillerist Captain Henry A. DuPont, who commanded the artillery in Crook's Eighth Corps, which was tasked with protecting the Union left flank, also believed, as he reminisced after the war, that the Union left was "very inadequately protected."[49] After the war General Crook also concluded that the Union left flank had been vulnerable mostly because of a lack of cavalry support to guard the fords along Cedar Creek.[50] Even some of the enlisted in the Army of the Shenandoah believed that the position—although difficult to take with a frontal assault—had a particularly weak left flank. On October 20, 1864, the day after the battle, an enlisted man in the Fifth Vermont observed that the position of the army left the flanks open "in a careless manner" and that weakness indeed "dared [Early] to attack us."[51] Gordon and Hotchkiss viewed the weaknesses that DuPont, Crook and others in the Union army perceived about the left flank. The two Confederates discussed the matter as they came down from the mountain, and Gordon agreed that he would take the intelligence to Early and push for an attack against the Union left.

The following morning General John Pegram—a division commander in Early's army—went to Early and urged an attack against the Union right flank. Early listened and then Hotchkiss informed Early that Gordon too had a plan to attack the Union position. Early's division commanders met at his headquarters at Round Hill on the morning of October 18 and decided how best to strike the Army of the Shenandoah. After conferring with his subordinates, Early determined to strike the Union left as Gordon and Hotchkiss initially recommended. The Confederate assault plan had four basic elements: First, Early decided to have the three divisions of Generals Gordon, Stephen Dodson Ramseur and Pegram attack the left flank. Second, Early ordered General Gabriel Wharton's division to move north along the Valley Pike. Next, Early tasked General Thomas Rosser with dealing with the Union cavalry posted on the Union right. Lastly, Early wanted General William Payne's cavalry to attack Belle Grove and kidnap General Sheridan, whom Early did not know at the time was not with his army.[52] While Early and his officers prepared for the attack, which would commence during the early hours of October 19, most Union soldiers still maintained their sense of confidence that Early's army would do nothing.

Although most Union soldiers believed that Early had been whipped and would not attack, some higher-ranking officers believed that Early still posed a tremendous threat. Brigadier General William Emory—affectionately referred to as "Old Brick Top" by his men—was perhaps the most anxious about the possibility of a Confederate assault. A veteran of the Nineteenth Corps observed that "Emory had for some days been distrustful of the excessive tranquility."[53] In addition to the "excessive tranquility," Emory received reports on October 17 that several Confederates appeared to be spying on the Union position from atop Signal Knob. Indeed, the reports Emory received were true as the men atop Signal Knob were Gordon, Hotchkiss, Evans and Hunter. Additionally, on October 18 one of Emory's brigade commanders, Colonel Stephen Thomas, reported that he saw two individuals who appeared to be spying on the Union position at the base of Massanutten Mountain. Although neither Gordon nor Hotchkiss ever made specific reference to this, a number of sources state that on October 18 Gordon and Hotchkiss donned civilian clothes so as to get close to the Union lines. Thomas could not rest easy with reports such as these and relayed the information to his superiors. "But while a sense of absolute security prevailed in camp the night before the battle," recalled a member of the Eighth Vermont, Thomas's old regiment, "there was one officer who had his suspicions that danger was close at hand, and, after making a personal investigation, he caused his fears to be reported at headquarters."[54]

General William H. Emory, commander of the Nineteenth Corps. *Author's collection.*

When Emory received this additional news from Thomas he promptly relayed it to General Wright. Emory appealed to Wright to do something and prepare for a potential assault. The temporary army commander, recalled a veteran of Emory's corps, considered the matter, but "did not think there was occasion for undue anxiety." In addition to the reports from Thomas, the Army of the Shenandoah's provost marshal—Benjamin W. Crowninshield—also stated that questioning of Confederates captured by Union soldiers in the days prior to the battle gave the sense "that some move was contemplated."[55] Furthermore Crowninshield reported that the Army of the Shenandoah employed thirteen spies who acquired information that corroborated the intelligence gained from the Confederate prisoners.[56] Despite the information presented to Wright, the temporary army commander did not appear to be too alarmed about a potential attack.

At approximately the same time that Emory expressed his concerns, Wright received a contradictory report from Colonel Thomas M. Harris, a brigade commander in Crook's Eighth Corps.[57] When Harris's troops returned from a reconnaissance on the evening of October 18, they reported to Wright that "nothing was to be found in [Early's] old camp and that he had doubtless retreated up the Valley." While the Eighth Corps' reconnaissance revealed that the Confederates had left their camp, Early's forces had not done so to retreat, but rather to begin their movement to strike the Army of the Shenandoah's left flank. Confronted with conflicting intelligence and an anxious corps commander in Emory, Wright ordered Emory to send out a reconnaissance force early on the morning of October 19 to determine Early's whereabouts.[58]

Emory sent orders to three brigades in his second division—Brigadier General Henry Birge, Colonel Edward Molineux and Colonel Daniel Macauley—to be prepared to move at 5:30 a.m. on October 19.[59] Despite Wright's order to have a reconnaissance sent in the morning some veterans of the Nineteenth Corps believed that it was done merely to placate Emory's fears, rather than for the army's safety. Something that supports the notion that Wright did not have tremendous anxieties about Early's intentions was that on the night of October 18—despite the conflicting reports he received about Early's army—Wright altered the course of an important order from General Sheridan. Before Sheridan left for Washington, D.C., he gave Wright direct instructions to have reveille blown at 2:00 a.m. and have the men under arms so as to reduce the chance of a surprise attack. After several days of inactivity Wright suspended Sheridan's order on the night of October 18 and allowed the men to sleep longer.[60] "Some suspicions were aroused," recalled a veteran of the Fourteenth New Hampshire, "but none at all of his real intent. Some unusual movement of Rebel troops was observed, but evidently General Wright was not in the slightest degree alarmed."[61]

In addition to the information presented to Wright by officers from the Nineteenth Corps, some soldiers in the Eighth Corps thought that around 10:00 p.m. on October 18 they saw lights flashing from the Confederate signal station atop Signal Knob as if they were sending signals with torches.[62] Although this was reported to Wright, he did not seem the least bit alarmed.

While officers such as Emory and Thomas stood vigil throughout the night, Early's army moved out of its position on Fisher's Hill to launch its surprise attack. At midnight Early issued orders to march. General Early informed all of his commanders that the army must maintain silence as the movement's success depended upon the element of surprise. "No drums were to be beaten," recalled a South Carolina soldier, "nor noise of any kind made…The most profound secrecy, the absence of all noise, from rattling of canteens or tin cups, were enjoined upon the men. They were to noiselessly make their way."[63] A Louisiana soldier recalled they "were put in light marching order, the men being divested of their canteens and everything that could rattle or make a noise so that they could get as near as possible to the enemy before the movement should be detected."[64] As Early's troops moved along quietly, most Confederate soldiers knew what was at stake with this attack, and some troops in Early's army were not only fighting for military reasons, but also for their homes and families in the Valley. Captain Samuel Buck of the Thirteenth Virginia, a regiment that served in Pegram's division, recalled that he had played on the fields and pathways along which Early's army now moved. "Every tree was familiar to me. As a boy I rode and walked almost daily through this section…I used to hunt squirrels and birds I now hunt men and the game is plentiful."[65]

Even as Early's army moved into position the majority of the Army of the Shenandoah, aside from some officers, went to bed with a profound sense of security that Early's army either remained in its position or had withdrawn from the lower Valley completely. "When, on the evening of October 18th, the last tap of the drum had ceased to call the men to sleep," remembered a solder in the 114th New York, "the boys little dreamed that the oft-defeated and badly whipped Early could possess enough elasticity and vitality to assume the offensive and renew the contest."[66] A soldier in the 110th Ohio, A.R. Rhoades, informed his wife on October 18 that the troops in his regiment believed that if Sheridan's army did nothing the Confederates "would fall back if we lay quiet."[67] A soldier in the 14th New

Hampshire echoed the feeling of confidence that permeated the majority of the rank and file in the Army of the Shenandoah on the night of October 18: "Probably no army turned into its blankets with a more perfect feeling of security than that which possessed Sheridan's troop's on the night of October 18. There was perfect confidence that Early had been so gloriously whipped that he would never dare attack the Union force in the Valley, and that his only purpose was to maintain a strong defensive."[68] Although most believed that Early would not dare attack, an assault against the Army of the Shenandoah appeared to be Early's only hope for survival. "The Army of the Shenandoah settled down in its fortified camp behind Cedar Creek with perfect confidence that it was secure from any successful attack by the forces under General Early," observed a veteran of the 121st New York after the war, "but that doughty warrior thought otherwise and planned to make one more attempt to win back his laurels as a fighter and strategist."[69]

Chapter 3

"Early's 'Good morning' salutation"

While a dense fog shrouded Early's army in an ethereal atmosphere during the early hours of October 19, soldiers from Captain Frederick C. Wilkie's Fifth New York Heavy Artillery picketed the left flank of the Army of the Shenandoah. Although these soldiers had no idea how the events of that morning would alter their lives, Wilkie and his men had an uneasiness about them during the night of October 18 and the early hours of the nineteenth. Throughout the night, as they picketed, the New Yorkers reported an excessive amount of noise coming from east of their position. Wilkie informed his brigade commander—Colonel Thomas F. Wildes—about this, but Wildes initially thought nothing of it. While Wilkie and his men wondered about the cause of the noise, it also caught the attention of the Thirty-fourth Ohio's Lieutenant Colonel Luther Furney. As officer of the day for General Crook's Eighth Corps, Furney decided to ride down to Cedar Creek to investigate. As Furney rode toward Cedar Creek he might have believed, as Crook stated after the war, that it was Union cavalry doing a reconnaissance mission; however, as Furney explored, he discovered that it was not Union cavalry, but rather the van of Early's attack column. The Confederates captured Furney, and unfortunately he had not been able to warn the Army of the Shenandoah about the Confederate advance.[70]

Around 4:00 a.m., however, picket fire sounded the alarm about Early's intentions as troopers from Brigadier General William H. Payne's cavalry fired into the Federal pickets near Bowman's Ford. After a short exchange of fire between the New Yorkers and Payne's horsemen, the Confederates withdrew. As the sound of small arms fire rolled into Thoburn's camps, Colonel Wildes immediately knew now that the sounds reported to him

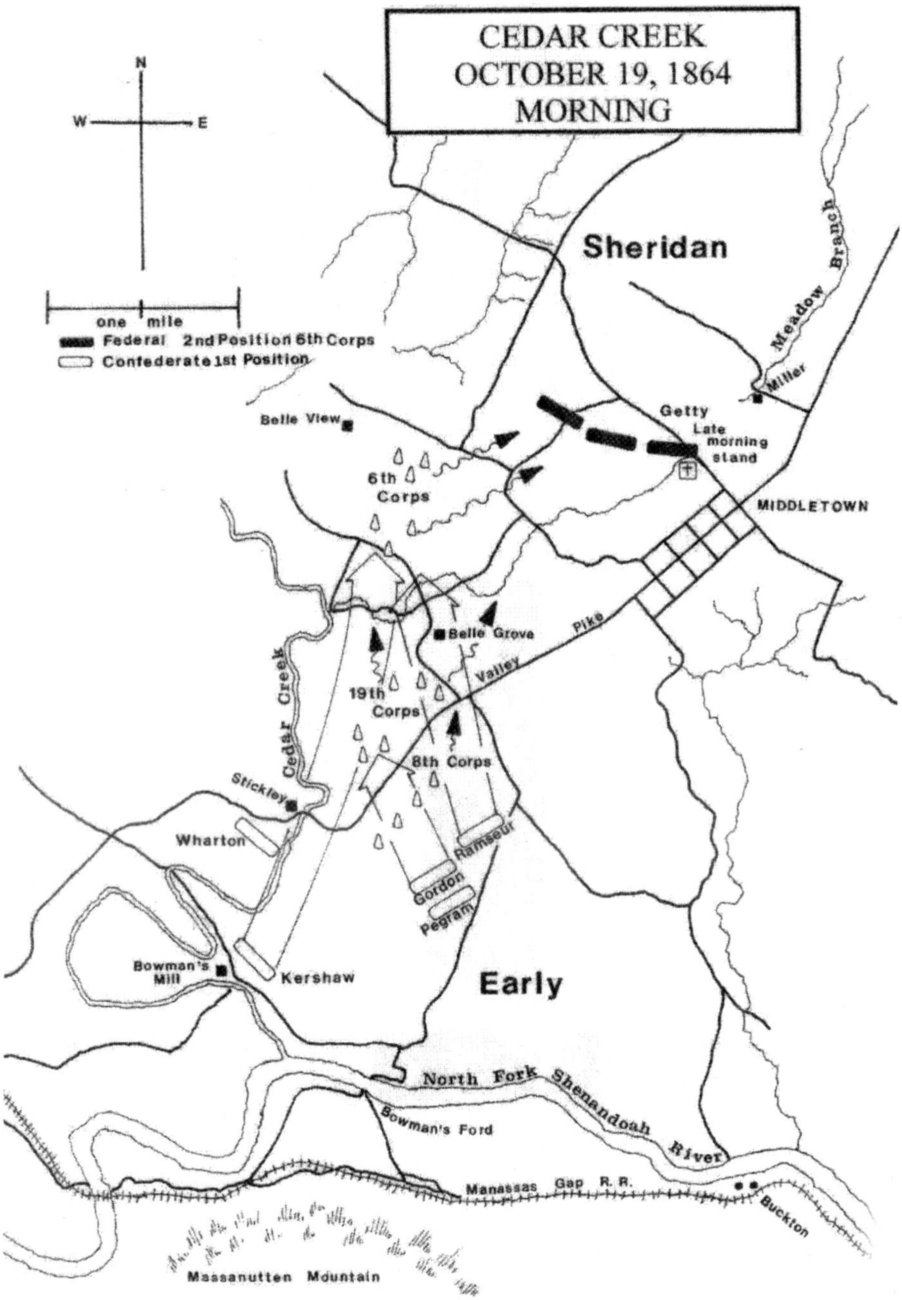

The opening phase of the Battle of Cedar Creek. *Map prepared by Blake Magner.*

earlier by Wilkie were the enemy. Not wanting to take any chances, Wildes reported that after he "heard brisk picket firing [he] ordered the brigade under arms behind its fortifications."[71] Although Payne's troopers pulled off the field, their exchange with Wilkie's men portended Early's planned assault against the Union left flank.

While Wilkie's men dealt with Payne's troopers on the extreme left, additional Confederate cavalry led by Brigadier General Thomas Rosser assaulted the extreme right of the Union line along Cedar Creek near Cupp's Mill. Around 4:00 a.m. Rosser locked horns with the pickets of the Seventh Michigan Cavalry. Soon the Seventh Michigan received support from the other regiments in their brigade, commanded by Colonel James Kidd. As Kidd's troopers mounted and launched a counterattack against their Confederate foe, additional cavalry from Brigadier General George Custer's division and Colonel Charles Russell Lowell's brigade arrived on the scene to support Kidd. Rosser now had no choice but to retire. His mission of creating a diversion on the Union right flank had failed. Some Union cavalry at Cupp's Ford seemed a bit surprised that after Rosser's troopers had been driven back across Cedar Creek, they did not reorganize and mount another assault. Custer, who had been a friend of Rosser's at West Point, noted curiously that after the Confederate force had been driven across Cedar Creek they did not appear to want to press the issue at Cupp's Ford and seemed "content."[72]

The gunfire that erupted early that morning also caught the attention of the civilians who lived in the area of Middletown. A young boy who lived at a home near Cedar Creek recalled that when he heard the fire erupt around 4:00 a.m. he was excited because he had never seen a real battle. As a border community, residents of the area saw armies come and go, camp and fight some small engagements, but never before had they experienced a real battle. "I'd heard a great deal about battles, but had never seen one, and my curiosity was excited," recalled the young boy.[73] In Middletown, the daughter of a free black man—Abe Spencer—also appeared excited at the prospect of seeing a real battle. At the first sound of fire, Spencer's daughter recalled that "ever'body in town had got up and lit their lights."[74]

Within an hour after the first shots on both flanks, General Joseph Kershaw's infantry division crossed Bowman's Mill Ford and slammed into the Union left flank. Kershaw's attack occurred with such speed and surprise that only forty men of the entire Fifth New York Heavy Artillery escaped capture during the opening infantry assault. The New Yorkers, recalled Wilkie afterward, were "unable to check in the slightest degree the advance of the enemy…with the exception of about forty men capable of bearing arms, the whole battalion was captured."[75]

With the pickets now swept aside, Kershaw's division assaulted the Army of the Shenandoah's left flank, held by Thoburn's division. Although the Confederates seemed confident going into the battle, some of them still wondered how they would crack Thoburn's fortified position. A South Carolinian in Kershaw's command regarded Thoburn's position as "the most completely fortified position by nature, as well as by hand, of any line occupied during the war."[76] Colonel James Simms, a Georgian who commanded the lead brigade in Kershaw's division, noted of the strength of the Union position, "The works were of a formidable character, with a strong abatis covering most of the front and in a favorable position for defense."[77] Despite the seemingly strong nature of the Union position, the army's strength could not be realized if troops were not properly placed to defend the position. Although Wildes ordered his men into line at the sound of the picket firing, the troops did not form quickly enough to meet the Confederate assault. Some men did not even have time to put their uniforms on, and as Kershaw's men neared the fortified positions, they saw "half-dressed Union troops" in the earthworks.[78] With the odds not in their favor, those half-dressed soldiers from Thoburn's division formed as best as time allowed and fired at their attackers. Some of the Confederates who struck Thoburn's position that morning viewed the fire from Thoburn's men as "galling" despite the disorganized nature of the Union troops.[79] B.F. Cobb, who served in the Tenth Georgia Infantry in Kershaw's division, recalled that as his regiment moved closer to the Union position, he could see Thoburn's men scurrying into line. He believed that if the Federals opened fire they would "catch it." Although the Union defenders only fired several volleys into their attackers, Cobb recalled that it seemed to him as if the entire Union division "opened fire on us from behind the breast-work, which made a solid sheet of fire in our front. That really done us more damage than all the balance of the days fighting…killed and wounded scores of our boys."[80] As Kershaw's men advanced, they sensed that a rapid charge needed to be made in order to drive the Federals from their earthworks. Kershaw's division moved rapidly forward "with one impulse"; however, the advance slowed when the Confederates came to abatis in front of the Union works. After a momentary halt to get on the other side of the obstacles, Kershaw's men pushed Thoburn's division rapidly from their camps and works. "We gave a Rebel yell and ran right

Above, left: General Joseph Kershaw. *Battles and Leaders*.

Above, right: Colonel Joseph Thoburn, killed at Cedar Creek. *Nicholas P. Picerno collection*.

in on them and scattered them like chaff before the wind," recalled one soldier in Kershaw's command.[81]

With Thoburn's infantry routed, First Lieutenant William Munk's Battery D, First Pennsylvania Reserve Light Artillery, tried to slow the Confederate advance. The Confederates closed within twenty yards of Munk's position when his battery unleashed canister on them. Still the weight of the Confederate attack overwhelmed Munk's gunners, who tried to defend their cannon with whatever they could. In the end all of Munk's efforts to defend the position and protect his guns proved futile as six of his guns were captured.[82] To make matters worse for Thoburn's men, the Confederates turned the captured guns on the fleeing Union soldiers. "We turned it on them," recalled a Georgian in Kershaw's division, "giving them grape canister shot and shells as they went over the next ridge."[83]

Approximately four hundred yards west of Munk's position stood the guns of First Lieutenant Henry Brewerton's Battery B, Fifth U.S. Artillery, who also tried to slow the Confederate onslaught. The difficulty that confronted Brewerton was that the fog prohibited him from knowing exactly where the enemy was located. Captain Henry A. DuPont, who commanded all of the artillery in Crook's corps, also could not see the enemy and ordered

Brewerton to simply fire a few rounds in the direction of the sound of the Confederate attack. Soon the Confederates swarmed around Brewerton's guns. Brewerton's Battery, despite the speed and surprise of the attack, fared a bit better than Munk and lost only one cannon. Brewerton, however, was not so lucky because he was captured trying to get off the field.[84]

By most accounts, within a matter of fifteen minutes Kershaw's troops swept Thoburn's division from its position. Thoburn's division, remembered a surgeon in the Twelfth West Virginia Infantry, "was completely surprised early in the morning, before day light by the rebels capturing our pickets and storming our breastworks, whilst we were all in bed. They jumped over our works with fixed bayonets, bayoneting and shooting down our men by the hundreds, before they could get fairly awake…to rally them seemed almost impossible."[85]

Thoburn's division suffered nearly six hundred casualties during the battle's opening phase. In the assault's aftermath a hellish scene of carnage replaced Thoburn's once peaceful camp.[86] Several children who lived close to Thoburn's position recalled that after fighting on the Union left flank subsided, they walked over the ground. The children noted that muskets littered the ground around Cedar Creek and that "the water was full of guns." The curious youngsters were awestruck by the gruesome scenes around Thoburn's position. "Soon we got to the battlefield, and we walked right along to the Yankee camp. Men had run out of their bunks who didn't get their guns at all, and we saw some soldiers in the tents who had been shot there. Some of 'em were dead. Behind the breastworks the dead and wounded were layin' five deep, and we waded through blood as we looked around," recalled one of the children. Not only did the scenes startle them, but so too did the sounds of wounded men's cries as they clung to life. "The wounded men were hollerin' and screamin' and prayin'. We heard one Southern solider prayin' for his wife and children way down in Alabama, and he was beggin' just for life enough to get back to see 'em. A doctor come along and examined him and moved on. He said there was no hope. It was sad," remembered one of the youths after the war. With such horrific scenes the children decided to leave the battlefield, but as they tried to make their way home they encountered Confederate surgeons at a field hospital operating on soldiers wounded in the assault. A young boy in the group noted that he witnessed surgeons "sawin' off limbs, and as soon as they got through with a man he was laid back on the ground where he'd been before. They had about a four-horse wagon load of limbs…in a heap just as you might pile up corn or manure."[87]

Colonel Rutherford B. Hayes. *Freedom Triumphant: The Fourth Period of the War of the Rebellion, 1890.*

When Kershaw commenced his attack against Thoburn's division, Thoburn's assistant adjutant general Lieutenant Frederick Ballard rode to the remaining division of the Eighth Corps, commanded by Colonel Rutherford B. Hayes, and informed him that they had been attacked. Hayes formed his division, which consisted of approximately 2,400 men, in line of battle a little less than one mile north of Thoburn's position. Hayes's line rested on the east side of the Valley Pike and along with Colonel J. Howard Kitching's provisional division on his left the Union line faced to the southeast to meet the Confederate assault. Shortly after Hayes and Kitching established their line they came under fire from General Gordon's division. As the Confederates advanced nearer, Hayes and Kitching started to take fire from the front as well as on both flanks. This fire signaled to Colonel Hayes that "the rebels were rapidly advancing."[88]

As soon as this part of the Union line came under fire, General Wright ordered Hayes to pull his division closer to Emory's Nineteenth Corps. When Hayes received this order, almost simultaneously the regiments on the left of his division began to break, partly because of Confederate fire, but also because of the panic created by Union soldiers streaming toward the rear from Thoburn's division. "Men, shoeless, and hatless," recalled a Confederate soldier in Kershaw's division, "went flying like mad to the rear, some with and some without their guns."[89] Confusion dominated the Eighth Corps despite the efforts of Federal officers to rally their troops. The pressure from the Confederate attack became too much for these men to endure. Colonel Benjamin F. Coates, who commanded a brigade in Hayes's division, wrote only, "Our division had not more than got in line when a most deadly fire was being poured into our ranks and a general confusion prevailed…

Our lines were being driven on all sides."[90] Under thirty minutes from the time Early launched his infantry assault, Crook's Eighth Corps—which had helped Sheridan win one month earlier at the Third Battle of Winchester and sealed Sheridan's victory at Fisher's Hill with a flank attack—succumbed to the enormous pressure and surprise of the opening Confederate salvo. A soldier in the Thirteenth Connecticut, a regiment in Emory's Nineteenth Corps, wrote that Crook's command had fallen victim to "Early's 'Good morning' salutation…The gallant Eighth Corps, which had won so glorious a name on many a battle-field…was now rolled up, trodden under foot, and swept away as easily as the whirlwind drives the autumn leaves. In twenty minutes from the firing of the first gun, the VIII Corps was a panic-stricken flying mob."[91]

In Cedar Creek's aftermath some soldiers in Sheridan's army looked with disdain upon the Eighth Corps for its performance at the battle. George J. Howard, a soldier in the 5th Vermont—a regiment in the Sixth Corps—wrote a letter home to his wife the day after the battle wherein he vented his anger over how Crook's command "foolishly" fled "before the rebs line of fire."[92] Reverend John Adams, the chaplain of the 121st New York, another Sixth Corps unit, wrote of the Eighth Corps' conduct on the day after the fight, "It was annoying, it was vexatious and humiliating, to see them turn their backs on their foe…startling from their sleep, the men were confused, and instead of forming into line, each one looked out for himself; they broke."[93] Crook's veterans took exception to this sort of criticism, which carried on for decades after the Civil War's end. One veteran defended the conduct of Crook's command and noted that any unit that held the position guarded by the Eighth Corps on the morning of October 19 would have been routed in the same manner, as they had no real substantial amount of time to organize any meaningful defense. "Had the Sixth been in place of it [the Eighth Corps]," the veteran concluded, "they would have acted similarly at Cedar Creek…The Eighth…were completely surprised, and we were compelled to fall back in confusion or be captured."[94] Captain DuPont wrote after the war, "No troops under the circumstances could have offered any effective resistance, but everything possible seems to have been done."[95]

Although the Eighth Corps did break rapidly, they put up as much resistance as possible, and all throughout the battle's morning phase the corps' various division, brigade and regimental commanders tried desperately to rally their commands. Colonel Thoburn frantically tried to collect the men of his broken division and paid for it with his life. As Thoburn attempted to reorganize his men on Church Street in Middletown Confederate cavalrymen—dressed in

Union overcoats and therefore able to get, as Colonel Thomas M. Harris stated, close "without exciting his suspicions"—shot Thoburn in the back and mortally wounded him.[96] Thoburn died from his wound that evening. The news of Thoburn's death saddened many, but the news arguably hit the men of the First West Virginia Infantry the hardest as Thoburn had been the regiment's first commander. "No nobler man died that day than Colonel Thoburn," stated the regimental historian after the war.[97]

Colonel Hayes likewise, although he did not suffer Thoburn's fate, made every attempt to rally his broken regiments. "Every effort was made by all the officers," Hayes penned, "whom I had an opportunity to notice, to prevent confusion and a retreat. In every regiment a considerable number of men continued to contest the advance of the enemy with determination."[98]

Additionally as the Eighth Corps' veterans streamed across the Valley Pike, Colonel Wildes reorganized two of his regiments—the 116th and 123rd Ohio—which had been among the first troops in Thoburn's division to feel the weight of the Confederate attack. When General Emory and General Wright saw the Ohioans they ordered the two regiments to charge into a ravine on the east side of the Valley Pike.[99] General Wright personally led the 116th Ohio into the ravine, but as the Ohio regiment advanced it confronted, according to Colonel Wildes, "a terrible fire and counter charge...which swept us back again to the pike."[100] General Wright received a bullet wound to his chin during the assault.

Regardless of the best intentions of the Eighth Corps' officers, Crook's command had been broken too much to establish any immediate and effective resistance. The burden of holding off the Confederate attack now rested upon the shoulders of the next corps in line—General Emory's Nineteenth Corps. Emory, who had been uneasy for several days prior to the battle about Early's intentions, had his fears confirmed when the first shots rang out in the early morning hours of October 19. Captain John DeForrest, a staff officer in the Nineteenth Corps, noted that at the first sound of battle he went to Emory's headquarters and found his corps' commander "just up, coatless and hatless and uncombed, shouting for his horse and orderlies. He was more exicted and alarmed than would have seemed necessary to an ignoramus in warlike matters."[101]

When troops from Emory's corps first heard the gunfire that morning, some of them thought that it was a reconnaissance, but few fathomed that it would be an attack against Thoburn's flank. A soldier in the 114th New York, a regiment in the Nineteenth Corps, believed that a Confederate attack against Thoburn's position "seemed almost beyond the range of comprehension, that the lately vanquished rebels would dare fall upon them in their strong position."[102] Despite the difficulty in comprehending a Confederate attack, soldiers on the Nineteenth Corps' picket line knew that this was no reconnaissance mission. When soldiers from the 128th New York, who manned what they called the "Stonewall Post" along Cedar Creek and west of the Valley Pike, first heard the opening shots of the battle ring out, the Nineteenth Corps' officer of the day, Colonel Alfred Neafie, informed the New Yorkers that the firing on their left was a "reconnaissance in force" that had been ordered by Wright that morning.[103] However, as the 128th New York's Lieutenant Benson recalled, "a sheet of fire burst forth, followed by the rattle of musketry and the shouts of the combatants, and announced the dawn of another day of bloodshed." Humorously, Benson turned to Colonel Neafie and asked him "in a joking way, if that was the reconnaissance."[104] Soon the New Yorkers found themselves confronted with fire from General Gabriel Wharton's division. As Wharton's men advanced to within thirty yards of the Union position near the intersection of the Valley Pike and Cedar Creek the Confederates reportedly yelled out to the New Yorkers, "Throw down your arms, you d[amned] Yanks." The New Yorkers refused to surrender and instead, as one member of the regiment recalled, fired "three quick volleys…into them at less than thirty yards." For the men of Emory's Corps who refused to believe that Early would not attack, the fire of the 128th New York sobered them quickly.[105] The New Yorkers pulled back to the Nineteenth Corps' main line, but unfortunately approximately twenty of them were captured by Wharton's troops.[106]

As the New Yorkers engaged the Confederates from Wharton's division, the members of the Stickley family, whose home sat on the west side of the Valley Pike and just south of Cedar Creek within yards of the 128th New York's pickets, woke up as Wharton's men and the soldiers from the Empire State clashed. Mary Stickley, about eleven years old at the time of the battle, remembered the opening of the fight and the plight of the New Yorkers: "We had been inside of the Union lines, and the first I knew of the battle Mother woke us children up to look out and see the Yankee pickets surrender."[107] As the fighting raged that morning, the Stickleys' house and farm transformed into a makeshift field hospital for soldiers of both sides. One of the Stickley girls remembered that "every room downstairs was full, and the yard outside was filled, too. They just lay on the floor or on the grass with maybe a blanket or overcoat under 'em. The surgeons took anything they could get in the house for bandages." Additionally, the Stickley farm became a makeshift graveyard. During the opening phase of the fighting the Stickleys noticed two Confederate soldiers carrying a wounded soldier into their front yard. The soldiers intended to get the wounded comrade some medical attention, but sadly, as soon as they passed the Stickleys' gate, the man died. The family soon discovered that all three of the Confederate soldiers were brothers. "The two who had been carrying the wounded man buried him in the orchard under an apple tree and put up a piece of pine board at the head of the grave with the name of the dead brother very neatly penciled on it," recalled one of the Stickleys. The two Confederate soldiers informed the Stickleys that after the battle they would come back to reclaim their brother's remains, but they never did.[108] Although the identity of the Confederate soldier cannot be positively identified, more than likely the soldier buried on the Stickley Farm was a soldier from Georgia, Jesse Helms, whose grave still rests on the Stickley property—currently a private residence.[109]

In addition to the picket fire from the 128th New York, the fleeing troops from the Eighth Corps alerted the Nineteenth Corps' veterans quickly to the enemy's intentions. "The awful conviction came to the mind in a moment that the Eighth Corps, so gallant in all its former engagements, had been entirely and instantly changed into a disorganized mass of stragglers. So silently and suddenly did they rush into their camp," recalled a soldier in the 114th New York, "that many were unable to arm or dress themselves, before they were compelled to seek safety by flight. They came running to the rear without hats, coats, or even pants. One gaze upon this dejecting spectacle satisfied our men that they were to endure a trial more fiery than any they had ever experienced."[110] Another soldier in Emory's command noted that Crook's men "doggedly determined to go to the rear. Many of them were only partly dressed, some wearing only underclothing," and none of them "heeded" the pleas of Emory's men to "turn back" or "make a stand."[111] With Crook's two divisions fleeing rearward Emory's troops now knew that the Army of the Shenandoah's protection fell upon their shoulders. A soldier in the 116th New York recalled, simply, "The position of the Nineteenth Corps was now very critical."[112]

Unlike their counterparts in the Eighth Corps, Emory's troops were better suited to resist Early's advance because General Cuvier Grover's division had already been awake and prepared for its morning reconnaissance. Francis Buffum, who served in Grover's division, remembered that the troops in the division woke up slightly after 3:00 a.m. and were "quietly aroused." The men cooked and ate their breakfast and took positions in their earthworks, which stretched for more than half a mile on the west

Colonel Edward Molineux. *Fred Molineux collection.*

side of the Valley Pike toward the Union headquarters at Belle Grove. While the first shots of battle that rang out sometime after 4:00 a.m. might have startled some of Grover's men it did not create pandemonium. "In the Nineteenth Corps all was alarm," explained a soldier in the Fourteenth New Hampshire, "but no confusion; certainly none in the second [Grover's] division. The men were all under arms...The worst apprehension was, that Crook had been attacked." Perhaps the most prepared brigade among all of Emory's command was Colonel Edward Molineux's. Molineux, who had been born in England and came to the United States at an early age, ordered his men to pack up their tents and prepare for battle even before Early launched his attack.[113]

Despite the readiness of his troops, Emory understood that the Confederate advance moved with such speed against the Union left flank that if he did not do anything to slow its momentum, his line would be next to crumble. In an effort to disrupt the Confederate tidal wave and allow enough time for the Union supply wagons situated near the Belle Grove mansion to withdraw north and give the Union Sixth Corps time to prepare a proper defense, Emory ordered Colonel Stephen Thomas's brigade, which consisted of four regiments—the 12th Connecticut, 47th Pennsylvania, 160th New York and 8th Vermont—to move out of their position in the Nineteenth Corps' earthworks west of the Valley Pike and move to a piece of high ground east of the Valley Pike. Thomas, a native Vermonter with a reputation as a hard-nosed fighter, now held the unenviable duty of blocking Early's attack columns. "Col. Thomas and his brigade were close at hand, and, just as the gray dawn revealed the terrible slaughter beyond," recalled the 8th Vermont's George Carpenter, "Gen. Emory ordered them to advance across the pike—a single, unsupported brigade—against the best divisions of Early's army."[114] The men knew that they marched into a losing situation, yet still they determined to carry out their mission against insurmountable odds. The "brigade knew why it had been sent there," recalled Carpenter, "and firmly met the shock on ground which could not long be held." Thomas's brigade rushed into their position and braced for the storm of the Confederate assault. As the brigade's four regiments took position east of the Valley Pike, Confederate fire seemed to greet them from every direction. "As the great drops of rain and hail precede the hurricane, so now the leaden hail filled the air," remembered a survivor from Thomas's command, "seemingly from all directions, while bursting shell from the enemy's cannon on the opposite hill created havoc."[115]

The weight and speed of the Confederate attack fragmented Thomas's line in such a manner that each regiment almost fought as independent units. At one point Confederates swarmed around the Eighth Vermont and threatened to capture the regimental flags—the worst fate that could befall any regiment. Confederate soldiers demanded that the Eighth Vermont surrender its colors, but the men of the regiment shouted back defiantly that they would "never" relinquish their battle-worn banners. "Amid tremendous excitement," recorded one Vermonter, "commenced one of the most desperate and ugly hand-to-hand conflicts over flags that has ever been recorded. Men seemed more like demons than human beings, as they struck fiercely at each other with clubbed muskets and bayonets." With bayonets and muskets at point blank range, the dead and wounded piled up around the regimental standards, but they did not fall into Confederate hands.[116] "Men fought hand to hand," remembered an officer of the regiment, "skulls were crushed with clubbed muskets; bayonets dripped with blood. Men actually clenched up and rolled upon the ground in the desperate frenzy of the contest for the flags…There was not much attempt at order. Not many orders were given. The men realized that they were in a terrible mess and fought like tigers."[117]

Regardless of the tenacity that Thomas's men exhibited, the casualties began to mount, and they realized that they could not hold their position any longer. After approximately thirty minutes—time enough for Emory to reposition his forces so that he could protect his left as well as his front—Thomas ordered his men to fall back as he knew it was "useless to stand against such odds; neither could such frightful butchery be endured longer."[118] The brigade suffered catastrophic losses. In the Eighth Vermont alone the regiment lost 106 men out of 159 engaged, including the loss of 13 of 16 field officers.[119] The carnage suffered by Thomas's brigade during the early hours of the battle troubled General Emory for many years after the war. When several hundred veterans of Sheridan's army came to the

Defense of the flags of the Eighth Vermont Infantry. *History of the Eighth Vermont Volunteers, 1886.*

Shenandoah Valley in the autumn of 1883 to commemorate the nineteenth anniversary of the campaign, Emory and Thomas strolled over the ground east of the Valley Pike where his brigade sacrificed itself. When the two came to the scene of the carnage Emory grabbed Thomas by the hand and told him, "Thomas, I never gave an order in my life that cost me so much pain as it did to order you across the pike that morning. I never expected to see you again."[120] Thomas's brigade performed an unthinkable feat at Cedar Creek that earned the respect of not only Union troops, but Confederate ones as well. Captain Jedediah Hotchkiss looked on in astonishment at the stand made by Thomas's command. In a letter Hotchkiss wrote to the regimental historian of the Eighth Vermont from his home in Staunton, Virginia, in 1886, Hotchkiss conveyed his sense of admiration of his former enemy: "Gen. Thomas's command must have been under most admirable discipline to have been able to rally and form, under such circumstances, and for a time successfully oppose the onward rush of heavy masses of Confederate troops flushed with excitement of hitherto unopposed success. Such a display of heroic fortitude by the men and by the leader of your command is worthy of the highest praise and admiration."[121] Thomas received the United States' highest military honor for his actions at Cedar Creek when he was awarded the Medal of Honor on July 25, 1892.[122]

Colonel Stephen Thomas. *Author's collection.*

The Nineteenth Corps reversing the trenches at Cedar Creek. *Battles and Leaders.*

While Thomas's brigade desperately tried to hold their position east of the Valley Pike, Emory and Wright met and conferred about how best to slow the Confederate advance. Wright, with blood streaming down his chin, suggested that Emory take more troops from his corps and hurl them east across the Valley Pike at the enemy. Initially Emory might have considered this option; however, when Emory saw the troops from the Eighth Corps fleeing their position rapidly, Emory believed that his corps could best slow the Confederate advance from its trenches—a much stronger defensive position than the exposed ground east of the Valley Pike.[123] What Emory did not count on, however, was that Gordon's division extended the Confederate right flank so much that Gordon's men actually fired into the rear of Emory's troops. With fire coming in from their rear, the men of Emory's command now realized their position could be defended only if they reversed their trenches. "We saw plainly that if we were going to use *this* line of breast works which had cost us so much hard work," recalled a veteran of the 116th New York, "we must get upon the wrong side of them."[124]

To confront this new challenge Emory quickly realigned his corps. Emory sent two regiments—the 156th and 176th New York from Colonel Daniel Macauley's brigade—along with the Iowa and Indiana regiments from Colonel David Shunk's brigade to leave the trenches and form a line perpendicular to the main Nineteenth Corps' line. Additionally Emory send Battery D, 1st Rhode Island Artillery, to bolster the center of the Union line. The remaining brigades of Emory's corps moved to the outer part of their earthworks and faced to the north. Emory understood, as did the soldiers in his command, that they had to make some sort of a stand to delay Early's attack long enough so that the remaining infantry corps in the Army of the Shenandoah—the Sixth Corps—would have enough time to prepare a defense. "A shallow, dry ditch on the outside of a trivial redoubt constituted the final hold of the Nineteenth Corps on its fortified camp. It was in the case of a man who has been pushed out of a window, and who desperately clings to the sill with the end of his fingers," recalled one of Emory's staff officers about the position of the Nineteenth Corps.[125]

As soon as Macauley's and Shunk's troops got into position they came under fire. In addition to the obvious problems, these troops confronted something else that concerned the officers on the field—dense fog. A heavy fog still covered the field at the time these infantry regiments moved into position, and the officers worried that if they opened fire blindly into the fog they might actually fire on retreating soldiers from Crook's command instead of the enemy. "In consequence of the dense fog, which existed at the time, the enemy advanced…with[in] a short distance…before we could distinguish whether they were friend or foes," recalled Colonel Shunk, "the more so, as we supposed them to be a portion of the Eighth Corps, and notwithstanding we received a very heavy fire from that direction we did not reply to it until they charged."[126]

When the Nineteenth Corps engaged the Confederates General Wright ordered Emory to withdraw from his position and form a defensive line on the right of the Sixth Corps. Emory, however, did not like the idea and stalled. One of Emory's staff officers believed that Emory rejected the order because "Old Brick Top" wanted to check the Confederate advance long enough so that his troops could "get out of our trap without being closely followed and quite routed."[127] With no orders to fall back from their position, troops in Emory's command fought fiercely. Colonel Edward Molineux, whose brigade stood on the outer part of its earthworks, recalled that "not having orders to retreat I stuck it out."[128] Lieutenant Colonel Alred Neafie, who commanded the 156th New York—which faced to the east—recalled that the Confederates poured "heavy volleys" into Emory's entire command. Much of the fighting during this phase of the battle involved a desperate hand-to-hand struggle. "In the haste of slaughter men could not reload," remembered one of Emory's veterans, "but fought with their bayonets and clubbed rifles."[129] On several occasions Confederate soldiers attempted to seize the colors of various regiments. Fighting around the colors of the 156th and 176th New York had become extremely fierce. The only option that the New Yorkers had to defend their regimental standards was to strip them from their poles.[130] Despite the ferocity and resolve of Emory's men, the weight of the Confederate assault compelled Emory's men to pull out of their position by 7:30 a.m. Emory's men were no longer able to "resist the rush of rebels…and sustain the murderous fire."[131] A soldier in the 3rd Massachusetts Cavalry, which fought dismounted at Cedar Creek as part of Molineux's brigade, noted how the brigades, despite their desire to hold, began to fold under the pressure from the attack. "One by one, the brigades of the Nineteenth Corps gave way. They could not stand before such a fearful storm," recalled a Massachusetts soldier.[132] "It was now time for us to back out of our hole," remembered the Nineteenth Corps' Captain DeForrest, "and we marched rearward sadly diminished in numbers, though not a regiment had entirely disbanded."[133]

Despite the Nineteenth Corps' ability to hold their position for more than an hour against seemingly insurmountable odds, after the war some Union veterans of the Sixth Corps depicted the Nineteenth Corps' involvement at

Cedar Creek as trivial. Colonel Joseph Warren Keifer, a division commander in the Sixth Corps at Cedar Creek, wrote after the war that "the Nineteenth shared the fate of Crook's corps, and was soon broken and flying to the rear."[134] Another veteran of the Sixth Corps echoed Keifer's assessment and stated simply, "The Nineteenth Corps did not fight, and left before they had made any effort to stay the rebels."[135] Other soldiers who served in the Sixth Corps stated that the Nineteenth Corps had been the victim of an "utter rout."[136] Assessments such as these of the performance of Emory's troops at Cedar Creek are simply incorrect and unfair. The Nineteenth Corps had not been routed from its position and suffered severely so that the Sixth Corps would have ample time to prepare for its resistance. "The Nineteenth Corps fought for an hour a stern, hopeless battle, against the crushing odds that were opposing it, till the dead and wounded were, in some regiments, as numerous as the living," recalled a member of the Fourteenth New Hampshire, one of Emory's regiments, "retiring only when it became evident that further defence of that line was useful...Every step the enemy gained...had been sharply contested and deadly won. Through fog, dismay, and confusion, the Nineteenth Corps had fought as well as men could in the midst of such dire adversity."[137] Another veteran of the Nineteenth Corps defended its service at Cedar Creek and stated that it "made a gallant fight until orders came to fall back."[138]

After the Nineteenth Corps finally pulled back from its position General Emory, along with General Crook, made an attempt to organize the remnants of their fragmented commands around Belle Grove—which served as the Army of the Shenandoah's headquarters. More importantly, the ground around the home served as the parking area for all of the army's supply wagons. The Federal commanders had to try desperately to secure those supply trains and get them off the field as quickly as possible to prevent their capture by Confederate troops. The defense around Belle Grove bought the army's quartermasters and commissaries about thirty minutes to get the wagons off the field. During that half hour, the fighting around Belle Grove became desperate. "A great many line and staff officers took muskets, and lay down in the ranks of the men," recalled an officer from Crook's Eighth Corps, "while all mounted officers used their holster revolvers. The position was held for over half an hour."[139] Some of the Union soldiers who defended the ground around Belle Grove also believed that their sacrifice "checked the advance of the enemy, and pushed him back a short distance."[140] Colonel Wildes believed that the fighting around Belle Grove had been "the very hardest and most stubborn fighting of the day."[141] The obstinate resistance

Belle Grove, headquarters of the Army of the Shenandoah. *Personal Memoirs of P.H. Sheridan.*

did protect most of the Army of the Shenandoah's wagons from capture. Although most of the army's supply wagons got off the field safely, not all did. An officer in the Nineteenth Corps reported that at least five wagons were lost to the Confederates and some of the army's animals killed or captured. Captain DeForrest of Emory's staff noted the heroic attempt of a body servant named Patrick who attempted to drive a cow off the field. Unfortunately both succumbed to the fire from Gordon's men.

What further complicated the situation around Belle Grove was the presence of approximately three hundred Confederate prisoners of war who awaited transport to a Northern prison camp. When the battle began, Captain Benjamin Crowninshield worried that these prisoners might turn on their guards or become defenseless in the midst of combat. Crowninshield promptly rode to where the prisoners were being guarded by the Twenty-sixth Massachusetts Infantry Battalion and found them "nearly ready to move and in perfect order." Regrettably, as Crowninshield noted, some of the Confederate prisoners had been wounded by fire from Confederate troops during the fighting around Belle Grove.[142]

As the fire swirled around Belle Grove the home's occupants—the Cooley family and their servants—tried to take refuge in the property's buildings.

"The poor woman and children who occupied this house remained shut up in it all day, cowering below the level of the windows for safety," recalled one Union soldier of the civilians' plight.[143]

While Emory and Crook tried to organize their delaying action around Belle Grove, General Wright turned to the only infantry corps that had not yet been engaged for support—the Sixth Corps, which was temporarily under command of General James Ricketts while Wright commanded the army. Regarded by some as the best of the three infantry corps in the Army of the Shenandoah, the veterans of the Sixth Corps, who fought with the Army of the Potomac for most of the war, seemed to welcome the challenge that stood before them on October 19. A staff officer from the Nineteenth Corps reportedly heard someone say "loudly and cheerfully" that "the bloody Sixth is going in. *They'll* stop these blasted cusses. They say that, by Jesus, *they'll* hold 'em."[144] A surgeon in the Seventy-seventh New York—part of the Sixth Corps—believed that all hope for any reversal of fortunes at Cedar Creek rested with the Sixth Corps. "The hope of the nation now rested with those heroes of many battle fields. Now that peerless band of veterans, the wearers of the Greek cross, whose fame was already among the choicest treasures of American history," the New Yorker recalled, "was to show to the country and the world an exhibition of valor which should tower above all the grand achievements of the war."[145] Initially Wright ordered his first and third divisions, commanded by Brigadier General Frank Wheaton and Colonel Joseph Warren Keifer, respectively, to move from their camps north of Belle Grove to support Emory and Crook. As Keifer's division—the closest to Belle Grove—moved out it marched toward Meadow Brook, a small stream that bisected the Sixth Corps camps with the rest of the Army of the Shenandoah. Wright ordered each division commander to send one brigade across Meadow Brook to support the troops around Belle Grove. As Colonel William H. Ball's brigade advanced across Meadow Brook toward Belle Grove, the troops from Emory's command withdrawing to the rear temporarily broke up Ball's command. "Ball's brigade was run through by the broken troops of the Nineteenth," recalled Keifer, "and it was feared for a time it could not be held steady."[146] Colonel Ball simply wrote, "A large number of the Nineteenth Army Corps passed through the line and broke its organization."[147] The brigade sent from Wheaton's division—commanded by Colonel William H. Penrose—suffered a similar experience. Both brigade commanders, without waiting for orders, withdrew their commands from around Belle Grove back across Meadow Brook.

Now the high ground overlooking Meadow Brook became a point where some of the Sixth Corps' regiments could try to slow the Confederate advance. The difficulty for Keifer's and Wheaton's divisions was that the overwhelming pressure from the Confederate attack did not allow them enough time to form one large continuous battle line and instead caused each division essentially to fight separate battles without any corps cohesion. "The complete isolation of the divisions of the Sixth Corps rendered it impossible for their commanders to know the real situation throughout the field," recalled Colonel Keifer, "and neither of them had any assurance of co-operation or assistance from the others."[148] Despite the difficulties, however, the two divisions held their ground north of Meadow Brook until about 8:00 a.m.

During the time that the Sixth Corps units held their position north of Meadow Brook, Colonel Keifer, who also had some Nineteenth Corps' units extend his right flank a bit farther to the west, ordered a bayonet charge into the attacking Confederates from Kershaw's division. Keifer recalled that he "ordered a general charge along the whole line…and the enemy was driven to the east." The division commander believed that the charge disrupted the Confederates so much that "complete success seemed assured"; however, when Keifer saw Brigadier General Benjamin Humphrey's Mississippi brigade overlap his line, he suspended the attack.[149] This was not Keifer's only concern. As his men tried to hold their position, he became uneasy about running low on ammunition. Officers from the division tried to guide mules with boxes of ammunition strapped to their backs to the Sixth Corps' troops "through the fog, smoke, and confusion" so that the Sixth Corps' regiments could continue to hold their position.[150]

Despite the best efforts of both Keifer's and Wheaton's divisions, the assault's pressure forced them to withdraw north through Middletown with the rest of the army. As those two divisions grudgingly gave ground, the hope of the Army of the Shenandoah now rested with arguably one of its best divisions—Brigadier General George W. Getty's second division of the Sixth Corps.

When Getty's division marched onto the field, it attempted to link up with Wheaton's division and extend that division's line farther to the east; however, Wheaton's troops, "at last routed in turn by the heavy force of the enemy thrown against it," according to an officer in Getty's division, "broke in confusion and fell back…Getty was now left alone upon the field."[151] Keenly aware that he could not hold the field himself, Getty pulled his division back to the area around the Middletown cemetery—a commanding piece of

General George W. Getty. *Slavery and Four Years of War, 1900.*

high ground west of Middletown that afforded the best immediate option for defense against Early's attack. Getty placed his three brigades—Colonel James Warner, Brigadier General Lewis Grant and Brigadier General Daniel Bidwell—in a line of battle atop Cemetery Hill. A Vermonter in Getty's division believed that the position taken up by his division "was on the whole an excellent one, however, notwithstanding there were no works, walls, or fences."[152] With Getty's troops in position, Brigadier General John Pegram's division launched the first attack against Getty's line. "The assault was not long delayed," recalled Aldace Walker of the Vermont Brigade. "The enemy charged in full line of battle...They pressed their advance with great determination." Despite the audacity of Pegram's troops, the first Confederate assault failed. Next Brigadier General Bryan Grimes's brigade attempted to break the Union stronghold, but without success. Grimes noted simply after the battle that the Sixth Corps troops atop Cemetery Hill "made a most stubborn resistance."[153]

With the first two infantry assaults failing against Getty's position, Early now decided to utilize his artillery to soften the Union position. According to some Union accounts, Early unleashed the fire of thirty cannons. "The rebels now concentrated a terrible fire of artillery upon our position, and shell from thirty guns flew," remembered a Vermonter in Getty's division, "screaming devilishly, over and among us. The men hugged the ground, being somewhat covered by the hill." After nearly half an hour of concentrated artillery fire, the Confederate infantry assault resumed. Troops from both General Gabriel Wharton's division and General Joseph Kershaw's division readied their infantry to break the Union line. While the fight for Middletown's Cemetery Hill continued, General Getty received word that General Ricketts—the corps commander—had been seriously wounded. Ricketts's wounding now put Getty in command of the corps and Brigadier General Lewis Grant in command of the division. Around 10:00 a.m. General Getty—who remained with his old division as it was the only one engaged by this point—spied another attack mounting against his position. Believing that his men might not be able to fend off another assault, he ordered Grant to withdraw from the position and move north of Middletown where the rest of the Army of the Shenandoah gathered.[154]

As the Union troops began to pull off Cemetery Hill, Union cavalry—which had been predominantly posted on the Union right flank—now began to make its way to the Union left. When troops from Brigadier General Wesley Merritt's cavalry division came into Middletown and neared the Valley Pike, they viewed a chaotic scene. As the fighting moved through Middletown, most of the residents of the small village sought refuge, while some curious types such as Abe Spencer's daughter—a free black resident of the town—wanted to catch a glimpse of the fighting. "Thar was shootin' all along this pike, and lots of bullets went through the upper part of our cabin, but I enjoyed it," recalled Spencer's daughter. Oblivious to the dangers of a battle, the young girl remembered after the war that she ran from her home to a neighbor's home on the opposite side of the street several times. "I was small and didn't understand the danger. I thought it was the finest thing that ever was," the energetic girl recalled after the war, "and my folks couldn't hardly keep me in…I wasn't a bit skeered, and I run across to the Wright's back and forth. Oh! I was busy as a bee. The bombshells was comin' over, and I jis' thought it was grand. One bombshell lodged right in our garden. It makes me laugh yet to think what a goose I was."[155]

Despite the excitement felt by Abe Spencer's daughter, Union soldiers tried to make their way north of town, where General Wright wanted to establish a new line. To help him in this task, Wright turned to Merritt and ordered him to halt the fleeing Union soldiers with his cavalry. Merritt's officers received orders to use whatever force necessary in order to stop the retreating Union troops. "The Federal cavalry…was ordered to the performance of the most difficult and most distasteful duty it had ever been called upon to perform, and one almost impossible to accomplish," recalled a soldier in the Sixth New York Cavalry, "that of checking our retreating infantry and forcing them back in line."[156] One of Merritt's brigade commanders, Brigadier General Thomas Devin, recalled the scene as his troopers neared the Valley Pike: "I found large numbers of the infantry retiring by regiments, companies, squads, and stragglers. With some difficulty I checked the rout at this point…it being necessary in several instances to fire on the crowds retiring, and to use the saber frequently."[157]

With the Union army withdrawing through Middletown by 10:00 a.m., Confederate troops from Wharton's division along with Colonel Henry P.

General Wesley Merritt. *Photographic History of the Civil War.*

Sanders's brigade from Kershaw's division pushed through Middletown. As they swept forward, they ran right into Merritt's troopers, who were supported by five artillery batteries. The Confederates had enjoyed success all throughout the morning; however, the Union cavalry provided a huge roadblock for Early's army.[158]

Early now ordered his army to halt and not pursue the Army of the Shenandoah any further. Early's decision to arrest his army's progress became, after the war, one of the most hotly debated topics among Confederate veterans who served in the Shenandoah Valley and is still the center of discussion among historians today. Some viewed it as one of the war's greatest military blunders, while others saw it as a military necessity. Early believed that his decision to halt the advance that morning was prudent. Although Grant pulled his division off Cemetery Hill, the presence of Merritt's cavalry on the Army of the Shenandoah's left flank worried Early tremendously. Keenly aware of the Union cavalry's ability to wreak havoc—as it had done at the Third Battle of Winchester one month earlier—Early decided not to press the advantage.[159] In addition to the strength of the Union cavalry, Early also did not believe that he had enough soldiers to continue the pursuit.

Since the beginning of the attack, Early's infantry ranks had been thinned by soldiers who decided to plunder the Union camps. When Kershaw's division launched the initial attack against the Union left, a number of regimental commanders noted that after the Federals had been driven from their position a sizable number of Confederate soldiers broke ranks to loot the Union camps. Captain D. Augustus Dickert of the Third South Carolina Infantry remembered that the troops in his regiment could not resist the temptation to investigate what the Union soldiers had left behind. "The smoking breakfast, just ready for the table, stood temptingly inviting," Dickert recalled, "while the opened tents displayed a scene almost enchanting to the eyes of the Southern soldier, in the way of costly blankets, overcoats, dress uniforms, hats, caps, boots, and shoes all thrown in wild confusion over the face of the earth…All this fabulous wealth of provisions and clothing looked to the half-fed, half-clothed Confederates like the wealth of the Indies."[160]

After the war, some former Confederates condemned the conduct of their comrades at Cedar Creek who decided to pillage the vacant Union camps. Two days after the battle a soldier in Early's army, Daniel Wilson, wrote from New Market that many of the Confederates in Early's command with "the Yankee line in full retreat" were "tempted by the luxuries of the deserted camps, they forgot their duty as soldiers and fell to 'plundering'—the army became a mob—an undisciplined crowd of plunderers."[161] Other soldiers in Early's army believed that assessments such as those made by Wilson proved unfair. Confederate John Worsham contended that many of Early's troops had been in such a deplorable state that they had no other alternative than to plunder the Union camps if they wanted to survive. "The world will never know the extreme poverty of the Confederate soldier at that time! Hundreds of the men who were in the charge and captured the enemy's works were barefooted, every one of them was ragged, many had nothing but what they had on, and *none* had eaten a square meal for weeks," Worsham stated after the war.

> *In passing through Sheridan's camp they had a great temptation thrown their way; many of the tents were open, and in plain sight were rations, shoes, overcoats and blankets…the temptation to stop and eat was too great, as they had nothing since the evening before, and they yielded. Others tried on shoes, others put on warm pants in place of the tattered ones, others got overcoats and blankets…in this way half of Early's men were straggling, and this accounts for this thin line in front.*[162]

In addition to his army's ranks being thinned by looting soldiers, Early believed he had to halt the pursuit because those soldiers who did not succumb to the temptation to break ranks and forage in the abandoned Union camps were in no physical condition to go further. "It was now apparent that it would not do to press my troops further. They had been up all night and were much jaded…I determined therefore," Early explained after the war, "to try and hold what had been gained, and orders were given for carrying off the captured and abandoned artillery, small arms and wagons."[163]

While Early stated that he stopped the pursuit due to the presence of Union cavalry, the plundering and the wearisome condition of his troops, some of the men and officers in Early's command did not agree with his decision to halt. Some Confederate soldiers, such as artillerist Private Henry Robinson Berkeley, believed that, despite their thinned ranks, they had the Union soldiers on the run and subsequently stared squarely at complete victory. "We drove them in great confusion for two miles beyond Middletown and had we not been stopped by our generals I believe we could easily have driven them to Harpers Ferry," Berkeley penned in his diary on the night of October 19, 1864.[164] Henry Kyd Douglas, who served on Early's staff, also did not appear to comprehend Early's motives for the halt. "Why we did not attack at once," Douglas recalled, "before they got over the confusion and demoralization caused by the surprise, I do not know. We had much to gain by taking the offensive." Despite disagreement with Early's decision, at least Douglas recognized that the army's disorganized state did create some problems. "True, our infantry had been scattered and demoralized in stopping to plunder the camps they went through," Douglas wrote, "and the temptation of food and the smell of cooking were too great for their famished stomachs to resist." Regardless of the reason for the halt, Douglas believed that Early's order to halt had been a fatal mistake even with the troops lost to plunder.[165]

Although some enlisted men and officers such as Douglas condemned Early, none criticized him more ardently than General John B. Gordon. After the war, Gordon recounted a conversation he had with Early late on the morning of the nineteenth. According to Gordon, in an encounter on the field Early informed Gordon that "this is glory enough for one day." Despite the success enjoyed by Early's army up to that point, Gordon wanted to continue the attack and press the Sixth Corps, but Early would not allow it. "And so it came to pass that the fatal halting," Gordon believed, "the hesitation, the spasmodic firing, and the isolated movements in the face of the sullen, slow, and orderly retreat of this superb Federal corps, lost us the great opportunity."[166] Lieutenant Randolph McKim supported Gordon's assertion after the war and believed that if Gordon had been in command "there would have been no check in the pursuit."[167] Regardless of the reasons for Early's pause the Confederate soldiers that remained with their commands used the opportunity to rest. E. Ruffin Harris, who served with the Fourteenth North Carolina, recalled that once the Confederate line halted just on the northern outskirts of Middletown, "everything in line was soon asleep."[168]

On the Union side—all throughout the morning—the soldiers believed that they had lost a great opportunity in the Valley and started to see their earlier successes against Early's army vanish. A soldier in the 114th New York witnessed a pall of depression hanging over the Army of the Shenandoah by late morning. "The time came when the Army of the Shenandoah, lately triumphant in victory, was in danger of annihilation, and was compelled to retire, humiliated by an undeniable defeat...The army was woefully shattered...Gloomily our men tramped across the fields," recalled the New York soldier, "depressed in spirits, languid in body, hungry, and thirsty. They feared that their former victories had all been rendered profitless by this one miserable defeat. They reflected what a crushing weight the news of this battle must fall upon the North, and they trembled for the Union cause."[169] The Thirty-eighth Massachusetts's George Powers echoed his New York comrade's sentiment: "At this time the battle seemed lost, and all the maneuvering in the Valley for the past two months thrown away."[170] The Twenty-ninth Maine's John Mead Gould lamented, "I thought of the blood that had been spilled for nothing and that another sacrifice must be made for the cursed valley and that the rebellion was not ending. In fact I got 'blue.'"[171]

What made some of the troops in the Army of the Shenandoah feel even more dejected was that this defeat happened in the absence of their army commander, General Sheridan. A soldier from Emory's command remembered simply that the men "expressed their regrets a thousand times, that General Sheridan had not been with them."[172] Sheridan had been oblivious to his army's ordeals, as he was in Winchester when Early launched his assault. "Little Phil" arrived in Winchester on the evening of October 18 and received confirmation from General Wright that night that all was "quiet" in the Union camps along Cedar Creek and that Sheridan could wait until the following day to join his army. Fully trusting in Wright's abilities, Sheridan bedded down for the evening in the Logan home in Winchester. The Army of the Shenandoah desperately needed their commander—but unfortunately at the time when his army needed him most, Sheridan did not know it.

Chapter 4

"What only such Generals as Napoleon and his kind have been able to do"

While the Army of the Shenandoah confronted disaster during the early morning hours of October 19, General Sheridan rested comfortably at the Logan house in Winchester. As the sun rose that morning Union troops in Winchester heard the distant firing of artillery.[173] About 6:00 a.m. an officer from the picket line in Winchester informed General Sheridan that he heard cannon fire coming from the south. Sheridan asked the officer if "the firing was continuous or only desultory." The picket officer informed Sheridan that the cannon fire was "not a sustained fire, but rather irregular and fitful." Initially Sheridan did not seem concerned by this report as he knew that a reconnaissance had been ordered for that morning and more than likely the "irregular and fitful" shots being reported were a result of that.[174] One of Sheridan's staff officers, General George A. Forsyth, noted only, "Little apprehension was occasioned by the report."[175] With little initial anxiety Sheridan tried to lull himself back to sleep, feeling confident that his army did not confront any major danger; however, as the minutes passed the army commander began to grow "restless" and could not relax. Sheridan got out of bed, dressed and ate breakfast. As Sheridan went through his morning routine, the pickets south of Winchester reported additional firing to Sheridan. "Little Phil" again inquired as to whether it was sustained or intermittent. The reports stated that the firing appeared sporadic. As Sheridan mulled over the intelligence, a sense of tremendous uneasiness entered his mind. "I…requested that breakfast be hurried up," Sheridan noted in his memoirs, "and at the same time ordered the horses to be saddled and in readiness, for I concluded to go to the front."[176]

After a quick breakfast, Sheridan mounted his steed, Rienzi, and along with his staff headed for his army in Middletown. As Sheridan rode through

Winchester, the town's Confederate women offered lewd gestures to Sheridan and his staff. "I noticed that there were many women at the windows and doors of the houses," Sheridan recalled, "who kept shaking their skirts at us and who were otherwise markedly insolent in their demeanor, but supposing this conduct to be instigated by their well-known and perhaps natural prejudices, I ascribed to it no unusual significance."[177]

When Sheridan reached Mill Creek, about one mile south of Winchester, he suddenly stopped. According to staff officer George Forsyth, Sheridan "leaned forward and listened intently." Then, without uttering a word, Sheridan dismounted Rienzi and "placed his ear to the ground." Again Sheridan said nothing, but as a staff officer recalled, Sheridan arose in a "somewhat disconcerted manner." Now Sheridan and his party rode about a mile farther south and took advantage of a piece of high ground next to the Valley Pike. As the band peered into the distance, they spied the Valley Pike packed with wagons trying to hastily make their way to Winchester. "They were seemingly in great confusion," remembered a member of Sheridan's staff. Sensing a looming catastrophe, Sheridan ordered General Forsyth to ride ahead and find out the reason for the panic. Forsyth encountered a quartermaster sergeant who informed Forsyth that the "army had been attacked at daylight, defeated, and was being driven down the valley."[178] With this news, Sheridan now dashed for his army. As Sheridan passed through Newtown, five miles north of Middletown, Sheridan caught his first glimpse of the battle's toll on his army. "The road was filled with ambulances containing wounded men," recalled a Union staff officer. "It was a gruesome sight to meet the eyes of a commanding general who, three short days before, had left it a triumphant host lying quietly in camp, resting securely on its victories, and confident in its own strength."[179]

As Sheridan neared the battlefield and the sounds and signs of a battle lost increased, he pondered what he should do to stem the crisis. Sheridan initially thought that he should reorganize his army and move it north to a defensive position closer to Winchester. After brief consideration, however, this did not appear to be the best option to Sheridan. He believed that a withdrawal toward Winchester would show no confidence in his army's ability to regain the ground lost during the surprise attack. Sheridan understood that perhaps the greatest asset any army commander could have was confidence in his men. "A General lacking the confidence of his men is in a precarious situation," Sheridan once informed a graduating class from West Point. "It is the soldier who makes us all."[180]

General Sheridan greets his troops at Cedar Creek in this etching prepared in 1889. *Author's collection.*

Among the first to greet Sheridan when he arrived on the field about 10:00 a.m. was cavalry commander General Alfred T.A. Torbert and then General Wright. When Wright, with his bloodied chin, greeted Sheridan, he provided a summary of the day's events. Quickly, Sheridan determined to reorganize his army north of Middletown and prepare for a counterattack. Sheridan's old West Point roommate, General Crook, liked the idea although much of Crook's command had been shattered during the early morning attack and would not be able to offer much help. "Crook…strongly favored my idea of attacking," Sheridan stated, "but said, however, that most of his troops were gone."[181]

While Sheridan began his army's reorganization his mere presence on the field seemed to instill confidence in his troops. As news of Sheridan's arrival spread through the ranks, the mood in the Army of the Shenandoah transformed from desperation to hope. An officer in the 29th Maine recalled of Sheridan's arrival, "There is no describing how that news affected us."[182] A veteran of the 159th New York echoed, "Sheridan immediately instilled new vigor, energy and determination into the men."[183]

Fully understanding Sheridan's inspirational qualities, a member of Sheridan's staff suggested that as the army reorganized Sheridan might consider riding up and down the lines, making certain that every man understood that the rumor of Sheridan's arrival was a reality. "I started in behind the men, but when a few paces had been taken I crossed to the front and, hat in hand," Sheridan remembered, "passed along the entire length of the infantry line…the officers and men…received me with such heartiness."[184] This gesture raised the spirits of the army as it reformed. "Sheridan possessed in a degree unequalled the power of raising the hearts of his soldiers, the sort of enthusiasm transmuting itself into action, that causes men to attempt impossibilities and to disregard and overcome obstacles," a veteran of the Nineteenth Corps recalled.[185] "The sight of the little man instantly inspired confidence in the men," penned a veteran of the 114th New York, "and threw them into a perfect frenzy of enthusiasm."[186] "The tide was turning. Riding over the field," remembered a soldier in the 38th Massachusetts, "showing himself to every regiment, and everywhere received with enthusiasm, the presence of a master spirit was at once felt."[187]

From their halted positions just north of Middletown, Early's Confederates heard the cheers coming from the Army of the Shenandoah in the late morning and early afternoon. Some had actually surmised that the cheers came from a sizable reinforcement of Union soldiers. An officer in the Thirteenth Virginia wrote, "While we lay waiting for orders, Sheridan was moving up from Winchester with a fresh corps that had not fired a gun, and with as many men as we had in our army."[188] Confederate artillerist Private Henry Berkeley believed that the Army of the Shenandoah had received a "large re-enforcement."[189] In reality, the army received no large reinforcement—just the confidence that Sheridan inspired. "A powerful enforcement had arrived," remembered a New York infantryman, "but it was only one man."[190]

Uncertainty now loomed among the Confederate high command about the condition and strength of Sheridan's army. Around 1:00 p.m. Early ordered General Gordon with troops from Clement Evans's, Joseph Kershaw's and Stephen Ramseur's commands to advance and test the strength of the Union line. Sheridan, from his vantage point near the Valley Pike, viewed Gordon's advance. Gordon's movement came at the most inopportune moment for Sheridan as he was in the process of making final preparations for his counterattack. "After re-arranging the line and preparing to attack I returned again to observe the Confederates, who shortly began to advance on us," Sheridan explained. Gordon's advance did not threaten the entire Union position, only the part held by Emory's Nineteenth Corps on the Union right.[191] At first Gordon deployed skirmishers to test Emory's regiments.[192] As Gordon's skirmishers neared Emory's line they encountered severe small arms fire. "There was an awful rattle of musketry," recalled the Nineteenth Corps' Captain John DeForrest, "which the forest re-echoed into a deep roar, and when the firing stopped and the smoke cleared away no enemy was visible."[193] A soldier in the 128th New York recalled, as the Confederate skirmishers drew closer, "On they came confident of crushing all opposition. Perfect quiet reigned within our lines until they arrived within about forty yards of us when the entire division [General Cuvier Grover's] arose and delivered their fire. The fire was frightfully effective. The enemy fairly staggered, attempted to rally, and finally broke and fled."[194] A Confederate soldier described the attack with less bravado: "They [Gordon] attacked at once, but so feebly and were so easily repulsed."[195] After the brief melee, Emory informed Sheridan that the Confederate attack had been "promptly driven back." The news pleased Sheridan, but Gordon's reconnaissance created uncertainty in Sheridan's mind about Early's intentions. Sheridan informed Emory that should the Confederates assault his position again "to go after them, and to follow them up, and to sock it to them, and to give them the devil."[196]

Neither Emory nor any other Union commander would have to worry about another assault from Early's army. After the rapid repulse of Gordon's skirmishers, Gordon decided not to launch the attack. Now Early decided that his army had indeed done enough fighting for one day. "The advance was made for some distance, when Gordon's skirmishers came back reporting a line of battle in front behind breastworks," Early explained, "and...It was now apparent that it would not do to press my troops further."[197] Early believed that he probably had more to lose than gain by pressing the Union line, as he recognized that his army was tired, the ranks disorganized from the morning assault and, furthermore, the Army of the Shenandoah now appeared to be in a strong position. After the war, a Confederate veteran who fought at Cedar Creek, Captain J.S. McNeilly, found little fault with Early's decision to not pressure the newly reformed Union line, especially after Gordon's repulse. McNeilly, like Early, not only feared the new Union infantry position, but also what Sheridan's cavalry might do should the Confederates launch another assault. Although many of Early's critics such as General Gordon did not address this point after the war in condemnation of Early's conduct at Cedar Creek, by the time of Cedar Creek, Early's troops appreciated the fighting ability and tenacity of the Union cavalry, and some believed that to advance against the cavalry would achieve nothing. McNeilly simply observed that the mere presence of the Union cavalry and its record during Sheridan's 1864 Shenandoah Campaign "decided the day that begun in triumph and ended in gloom."[198]

While some Confederates lamented Early's decision to not continue the assault, Sheridan confronted a dilemma of his own that afternoon: Did Early have reinforcements on the way? Sheridan still worried about the possibility of reinforcements from General James Longstreet's corps being present to support Early. Although the reports that Sheridan had about reinforcements from Longstreet proved fictitious after the battle, on the afternoon of October 19, he did not know about their validity and wanted confirmation before he struck his nemesis. Sheridan turned to General Merritt and ordered him to attack "an exposed" Confederate artillery battery and take some prisoners for questioning. "Merritt soon did this work effectually, concealing his intention till his troops got close in to the enemy," Sheridan recalled, "and then by a quick dash gobbling up a number of Confederates." Sheridan briefly interrogated the Confederate prisoners about the presence of reinforcements. They informed Sheridan that the only troops from Longstreet's command attached to Early's army were Kershaw's division. While this news initially pleased Sheridan, he soon received information that Longstreet was marching via the Front Royal Road toward Winchester where he would attack the rear of the Army of the Shenandoah. "This renewed my uneasiness," Sheridan wrote, "and caused me to delay the general attack." However, once Colonel William Powell, whose troopers protected that approach to Winchester, informed Sheridan that Longstreet was nowhere to be found Sheridan now decided to attack Early's position.[199]

As Sheridan's confidence was bolstered by Powell's report, doubt among Confederate soldiers on Early's left flank increased. According to General Gordon, at some point around 3:00 p.m. he received reports from the Confederate signal station atop Signal Knob as well as from General Thomas Rosser that Sheridan was massing heavy forces against the Confederate left. "The flag signals from the mountain and the messages from Rosser became more intense in their warning…Sheridan's marchers were coming closer and massing in heavy column on the left, while his cavalry were gathering on our flank and rear," Gordon explained. Armed with this news, Gordon appealed to Early for additional men to bolster the left flank. General Early informed Gordon that he did not have any reinforcements to send, aside from some additional artillery support. This enraged Gordon, who believed that Early "did not share in the apprehension manifested by the warning signals as to the danger which immediately threatened us." The only advice, according to Gordon, that Early provided was "to stretch out the already weak lines and take a battery of guns to the left." Following his meeting with

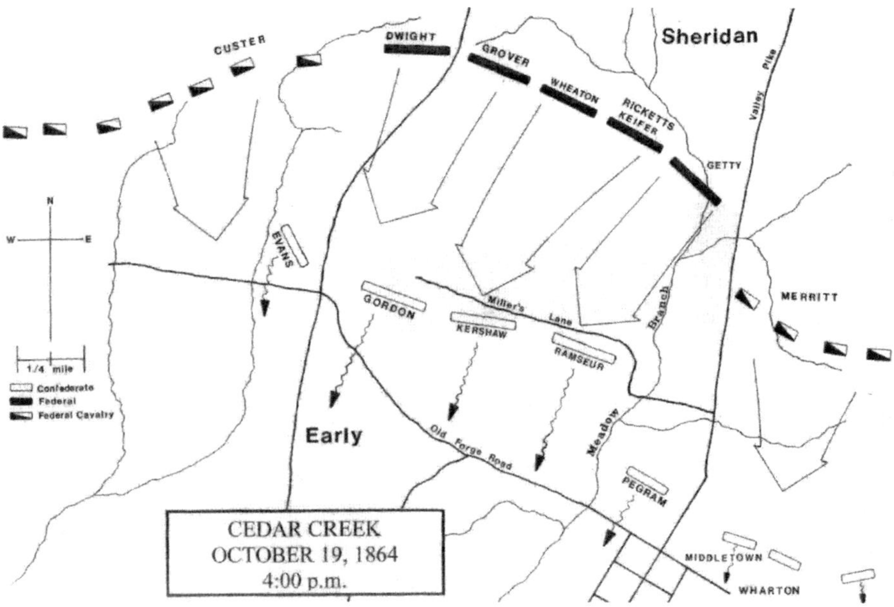

The Union counterattack during the afternoon of October 19, 1864. *Map prepared by Blake Magner.*

Early, Gordon rode back to his lines, but by that point Gordon recalled that it "was too late," as Sheridan's army had already started its advance.[200]

Around 4:00 p.m. Sheridan ordered the counterattack to commence. As officers shouted orders and bugles sounded the attack, Sheridan's men understood they now had the opportunity to erase the morning's disaster. "At four p.m. the command was sent along the line to prepare for a general forward movement," recalled an Ohioan. "Everything was soon ready; two hundred bugles sounded the advance; all our artillery opened on the enemy with shot and shell, and the long line of cavalry and infantry moved steadily forward."[201] As the attack commenced, Sheridan's soldiers understood the moment's significance. "We knew the time had come again," recalled the Twenth-ninth Maine's John Mead Gould, "once more there was a feeling of 'goneness' in our stomachs, but in full faith that Sheridan was managing rightly, we stepped over our rude protection and advanced."[202] A soldier in the Eighth Vermont wrote of the moment, "It was now life or death, and every man knew it. The order was instantly obeyed…and [we] moved rapidly to the front…Sheridan was riding furiously among the troops. Regimental officers were shouting their commands, and the hideous rebel yell rent the air and added to the general confusion."[203]

As the Union line surged forward, cavalry from General Merritt's division struck the Confederate line first on the east side of the Valley Pike. The stalwart defense of Wharton's division stymied the Union assault and forced it back.[204] To the right of Merritt's division advanced the Sixth Corps, which initially did not fare much better against the portion of the Confederate line held by Ramseur's and Pegram's division. A veteran of the Sixth Corps wrote, "The long thin line of the Sixth Corps was thus hurled against a very heavy line of the enemy, covered throughout by a series of stone walls." The Confederates maintained a steady fire and for the moment pinned down the regiments of the Sixth Corps.[205] "The rebels stood manfully, and repulsed all attacks for a while," recalled a Union officer, "realizing that all now depended on their holding their ground."[206] Colonel Keifer initially recalled that the Confederates were "obstinate and, for a time, promised to extend [the battle] into the night."[207] The intense volleys from Ramseur's and Pegram's commands actually caused some regiments from the Sixth Corps to fall back; however, the Vermont Brigade and elements of Colonel James Warner's brigade (both brigades served in General Getty's division) did not give way, although halted by the Confederate fire. "Although brought to a halt," a veteran wrote that these two brigades "stood firm, and with the utmost coolness opened so well-sustained and effective a hail of musketry upon the gray forms crouching behind the stone walls in front, that their fire visibly slackened."[208]

The preliminary successes of Early's troops in halting Sheridan's counterattack strengthened Early's confidence. Early believed that Sheridan's opening attacks were "handsomely repulsed" and caused Early to believe "that the day was finally ours."[209] While Early's certainty initially soared, the Federal line had not yet struck the Confederate left flank—the weakest portion of his line. As had been the case at the Third Battle of Winchester and Fisher's Hill, Early's left flank was vulnerable, and therefore became the focal point for the attack.

As troops from the Sixth Corps and Merritt's cavalry division struggled to break the Confederate line, troops from General Emory's Nineteenth Corps targeted Early's susceptible left flank. Emory's First Division, commanded by General William Dwight, who assumed command of the division that afternoon after Sheridan released him from arrest, advanced into a gap in the Confederate line.[210] Unbeknownst to the Union officers of Emory's corps, General Clement Evans's brigade was posted on a ridge on the Confederates' extreme left. Once Dwight's men entered the gap, Evans's brigade unleashed a furious fire of musketry into the right flank of the Nineteenth Corps. General James McMillan, who had temporarily commanded the division at Cedar Creek earlier in the day, wrote that as Dwight's division entered an open field, they "encountered a most murderous fire from a hidden enemy on the right and rear."[211] Once into the gap the Nineteenth Corps' veterans could see Evans's brigade. The Twenty-ninth Maine's John Mead Gould noted, "We could see one flag in particular waving defiance…That General [Evans] was mounted and gallantly leading his two little skeletons…and poured a tremendous fire upon our…flank."[212] With Evans's fire wreaking havoc on the Union right, McMillan's Second Brigade, along with two regiments from Colonel Edwin Davis's First Brigade, wheeled to the right and formed a line perpendicular to the main Union line to confront the Confederate fire. The Union regiments then surged forward into the Confederate attackers. "The enemy's fire was rapidly returned, the men firing at will, when… the brigade with shouts and yells charged…The enemy broke in great confusion and ran to the south and west," recalled a soldier in McMillan's command.[213] Another Nineteenth Corps' veteran wrote of McMillan's maneuver, "McMillan's brigade…by a brilliant counter-charge cut off the Rebel brigade [Evans] from the rest of the enemy's line, and sent it scampering away across Cedar Creek to our right, broken and useless."[214] After the war, Early believed that the failure of Evans's brigade to maintain its position spelled the imminent defeat of the Confederate forces.[215]

Following the Nineteenth Corps' initial success, Sheridan not only rode onto the field and shouted words of encouragement to Emory's men, but also advised the veterans to not press the Confederate line any further until Custer's cavalry division arrived to support the attack. "You are doing splendidly, but don't be in too much haste," Sheridan informed the Nineteenth Corps' soldiers. "Now lie down right where you are, and wait until you see General Custer come down over those hills and then…by God, I want you to *push* the rebels."[216] Shortly after Custer's troopers moved into position, both Emory's men and Custer's cavalry surged forward. The rush of the cavalry attack did not allow the Confederates any chance for meaningful opposition. "This time the rebels offered scarcely any resistance," recalled a soldier in the 114th New York, "but at the first onset broke and ran like a herd of stampeding cattle."[217] An officer in the 116th New York wrote that before the line surged forward he could see "the bright and glistening sabres" of Custer's troops and that the "suddenness of our onset made resistance impossible, and they fled before us, thus exposing the flank of the main line, upon which we now poured down with a still

General George A. Custer. *Battles and Leaders*.

fiercer shout."[218] Custer noted simply that, under the shock of his attack, the Confederate left "now gave way in the utmost confusion."[219] General Gordon, who witnessed the onslaught, recalled that the combined Union attack of the Nineteenth Corps and Custer's troopers caused the left flank to roll up "like a scroll."[220] Despite the success of this joint attack, some veterans of Emory's corps believed after the war that Custer received too much credit for their role in breaking Early's left at Cedar Creek. Francis Buffum, a veteran of the 14th New Hampshire and its regimental historian, asserted after the war, "It is a popular delusion that the cavalry initiated the rout of the enemy. The cavalry only finished a job which the infantry alone had begun."[221] Despite the postwar arguments that raged over how credit for the success should be doled out—not an uncommon phenomenon in postwar years as veterans thought about their legacy—it was indeed this combined attack of infantry and cavalry that prevented Gordon's command from erecting a stout defense.

After Gordon's position collapsed, panic spread epidemically throughout the regiments on the Confederate left. "To the surprise of Genl. Early the left suddenly gave way with the cry of 'we're flanked' 'we're flanked,'" recalled Confederate soldier Daniel Allen Wilson two days after the battle. "The panick [*sic*] spread along the entire line and the brave and gallant troops of the morning ran like scared sheep and soon in less time than it takes me to write it the army melted away into a chaotic mass of stragglers."[222] Early likewise believed that the panic that spread among his command was unnecessary and contributed tremendously to his army's defeat. "The information of this affair," Early concluded about the collapse of Gordon's line, "with exaggerations, passed rapidly along Kershaw's and Ramseur's lines, and their men, under the apprehension of being flanked, commenced falling back in disorder, though no enemy was pressing them, and this gave me the first intimation of Gordon's condition."[223]

"What only such Generals as Napoleon and his kind have been able to do"

Steeled by the success of the Nineteenth Corps and Custer's division, the remainder of Sheridan's troops pressed the enemy, but still seemed to confront stiff opposition on parts of the field. When Kershaw's division broke, Ramseur ordered his division to pull out of line and form on a hill several hundred yards behind his original line along Miller's Lane. When Ramseur pulled out of position, troops from the Union Sixth Corps immediately occupied the stone walls and buildings that offered protection for Ramseur's initial line. "The group of buildings from which the enemy fled…to a wall which protected their second line, was as good a protection for us as it had been for the rebels," recalled a member of the Vermont Brigade.[224] Although Ramseur pulled out of his main line and the Union attackers now had some cover, Ramseur did not intend to quit the field without a fight. General William Cox, who commanded one of Ramseur's brigades, noted that during this phase of the battle, "no man could have behaved more magnificently and heroically than Ramseur did in his efforts to resist the overwhelming tide which was now setting upon us."[225] Perhaps Ramseur fought with such tenacity and desperation at Cedar Creek because he hoped that a Confederate victory would allow him a furlough to return home to North Carolina to see his newborn daughter. Unfortunately, during Ramseur's attempts to thwart the Union attack, he was mortally wounded when a bullet entered his right side, pierced both lungs and lodged in his left side. When Ramseur fell, Major R.R. Hutchinson, who served as Ramseur's adjutant general, ran over to his wounded general and along with several other men carried him to the rear. They eventually placed Ramseur's mortally wounded body in an ambulance set to carry him south. Early wrote of Ramseur's conduct at Cedar Creek and subsequent wounding, "He fell at his post like a lion at bay, and his native State has reason to be proud of his memory."[226]

General Stephen D. Ramseur. *Battles and Leaders*.

As the Union assault swept the divisions of Gordon, Kershaw, Ramseur and Pegram from the fields west of the Valley Pike, Wharton's division still remained east of the Valley Pike. Undoubtedly inspired by their success throughout the day in keeping Merritt's troops in check, the Confederates braced for the assault. Wharton's gunners loaded their cannon with double-canister and unleashed a furious fire on Merritt's troopers. "The charge was made on an enemy well formed, prepared to receive it with guns double-shotted with canister," Merritt recalled. "Into that fearful charge rode many a noble spirit who met his death."[227] Still, it did not prohibit the success of the Union attack, and Wharton's division had no other alternative but to withdraw.

Among the Union casualties in Merritt's final attack was Colonel Charles Russell Lowell, who commanded one of Merritt's brigades. Lowell had been wounded earlier in the day and spent the early afternoon trying to regain his strength. When he heard the orders for the counterattack, Lowell informed the officers around him, "I feel well, now." With assistance from his staff, Lowell mounted his horse, but "could not speak above a whisper." As Lowell's brigade charged into Wharton's division and pushed them into Middletown, Lowell received a fatal wound. His men carried him to a house in Middletown where he clung to life. One soldier noted of Lowell's final moments, "He gave no sign of suffering; his mind was perfectly clear, calm and cheerful, he knew he had no chance of life. He dictated private messages of affection, gave complete directions to his command, and as the day rose he ceased to breath the air of earth."[228] General Merritt penned of Lowell's death, "His last breath was warm with commendations of his comrades in arms and devotion to his country's cause. Young in years, he died too early for his country, leaving a brilliant record for future generations, ending a career which gave bright promise of yet greater usefulness and glory."[229] To the Northern press, Lowell's performance at Cedar Creek and subsequent death came to symbolize patriotic fervor. *Harper's Weekly*, although understanding that Lowell's death caused sadness to his loved ones, believed that neither he nor any other Union soldier killed at Cedar Creek had lost their life in vain. "They die, these brave and noble boys, but they live," *Harper's* wrote. "They live in our purer purpose, in our firmer resolution, in the surer justice of the nation. Against compromise, against concession, against surrender, this precious blood cries from the ground."[230]

By 5:30 p.m., the Union assault fractured the Confederate line and sent the Confederate soldiers fleeing south. A veteran of the 122nd Ohio noted that "by half past five o'clock" the Confederate line "had dissolved into fleeing fragments." Some Confederates attempted to establish pockets of resistance, but all efforts proved futile.[231] Union troops surged forward and maintained a rapid fire. Sheridan's men exhausted their ammunition supplies quickly and

Colonel Charles Russell Lowell. *Memoirs of the War of '61, 1920.*

were forced to take ammunition from the wounded and dead.[232] As the Army of the Shenandoah pushed the Confederates through Middletown to the banks of Cedar Creek, the army lost its organization, but still each soldier understood the importance of success and pressed south. "Our formation was entirely lost but we had the organization and enthusiasm of recognized success," recalled a Vermonter.[233] A veteran of the 14th New Hampshire wrote of the pandemonium in both armies, "Every thing on legs was getting into a dead run; and both armies were full bent toward the pike crossing of Cedar Creek, neither Sheridan's nor Early's troops much regarding order: the one in a gallop of fun and boundless hilarity; the other panic-stricken."[234]

As the Confederates crossed Cedar Creek, some attempted a stand on the high ground above the creek near the Stickley Farm, but again all attempts proved useless as it became impossible to stop the Union tidal wave. A veteran of the Sixth Corps noted that, as they pursued to Cedar Creek, the Confederates "made a final attempt…to organize a last resistance on the hills that crowned Cedar Creek, but after a feeble volley the line melted away; a last battery faced us with a round of canister, but in vain."[235]

When Early's soldiers came rushing, panic-stricken, to the rear, Confederate doctors took action to evacuate the wounded and to prevent their medical supplies from falling into Union hands. Doctors who utilized the Stickley Farm destroyed what they could not carry. Mary Stickley recalled, "The surgeons set fire to the medical wagons and hurried off. Some of the wagons were down on the meadow and by the springhouse, and some up the hill back of the orchard. The chemicals in them made a bright blaze."[236]

While the Union infantry pursuit lost momentum by the time it reached Cedar Creek, Union cavalry, most notably troopers from General Custer's division, continued to push the enemy. The chaos of Early's retreat turned into catastrophe when a bridge over a small stream just south of Strasburg became clogged so that nothing Early had on wheels could continue the retreat south. Although there are several variations on what prompted this bridge to be clogged and impassable, the one account that is oft-repeated stated that two of Early's wagons tried simultaneously to get across and got wedged on the bridge.[237] An officer from Kershaw's division noted of this most unfortunate episode, "But in the rush some wagons got interlocked and were overturned midway at the bridge, and completely blocked the only crossing for miles above and below…In the small space of one or two hundred yards stood deserted ambulances, wagons, and packs of artillery mules and horses, tangled and still hitched, rearing and kicking like mad."[238] With the bridge clogged, many of Early's Confederates simply waded across the stream and regrouped at Fisher's Hill. Fleeing soldiers, a clogged bridge and Union cavalry thundering up the Valley Pike in pursuit of the Confederates created a complete scene of pandemonium. "The whole vast plain in front and rear was dotted with men running for life's sake," observed a South Carolinian, "while over and among this struggling mass the bullets fell like hail. How any escaped was a wonder to the men themselves."[239] While some Confederates got away, scores of Early's men were captured near the bridge as they could not outrun the Union horsemen. "I never saw such a stampede," recalled a Union trooper, "whole companies surrender to half a dozen mounted men."[240]

Among those captured was the mortally wounded General Ramseur. Corporal Frederick Lyon of the First Vermont Cavalry halted and captured the ambulance that carried Ramseur's body. According to a Confederate account, when the Union cavalryman asked who was inside the wagon, the driver simply told him, "The General says I must not tell."[241] Lyon, on the other hand, never stated that this is how he discovered it was Ramseur inside of the wagon. According to Lyon he heard a "voice from out of the darkness…General Ramseur is inside and he ordered us to 'move on.'" Certainly the opportunity to capture a general excited Lyon. The Vermonter maintained his "presence of mind" and ordered the wagon to halt and turn around for army headquarters at Belle Grove. A week after the battle, Lyon was ordered to Washington, D.C., where President Lincoln awarded the courageous cavalryman the Medal of Honor.[242]

When Ramseur arrived at Belle Grove, Union doctors, along with Confederate surgeon Dr. James Gillespie, tended to Ramseur's wounds. The doctors, according to one of Ramseur's staff officers who was with him, "did all that could be done under the circumstances." Some of Ramseur's old West Point friends including Custer, Merritt and DuPont visited him.

When DuPont approached Ramseur's deathbed, Ramseur extended his hand and grabbed DuPont's. The artillery officer confessed that he had been "deeply moved" by this and that, at that moment, he did not view Ramseur as an enemy, but rather as a friend: "Strange as it may seem—illogical, if you please—in that supreme moment he turned with content and satisfaction to the one person present who though officially a foe, was still, as he instinctively felt, the steadfast personal friend of former days."[243] Other Union officers, including Sheridan, did what they could to alleviate Ramseur's suffering. During his final hours, Ramseur spoke "continually" of his wife and child. He whispered to his adjutant general Major Hutchinson to "give his love and send some of his hair to his darling wife." Ramseur also told Hutchinson that he regretted not being able to see his newborn child at least once before he died. At 10:27 a.m. on October 20, Ramseur breathed his last. Major Hutchinson wrote to Ramseur's widow, "He told me to tell you he had a 'firm hope in Christ, and hoped to meet you hereafter.' He died as became a Confederate soldier and a firm believer."[244]

Amid the excitement that permeated the ranks of the Army of the Shenandoah also came horror as men crossed over the field and took stock of the battle's carnage. Many of Sheridan's soldiers noticed that some of the Union dead had been stripped of their clothing. "During the advance we found many dead comrades," recalled a member of the 1st Rhode Island Light Artillery, "stripped of their clothing, and this sight roused us to still greater exertions."[245] A veteran of the 121st New York noted of the horrible scene, "We went over the ground the Rebels had taken, and it was an awful sight. They had stripped our dead and wounded." The surgeon of the 77th New York recalled vividly of the macabre scene, "The moon shining brightly over the battle-field revealed the camps of the living side by side with the resting places of the dead. All the way from Middletown to Cedar Creek the debris of battle was scattered over the fields. Here and there were seen the remains of our comrades of the morning, their lifeless bodies stripped by vandal rebels of almost every garment."[246] Although some Union soldiers might have initially concluded that Confederate soldiers had been the ones who plundered the dead, some veterans suggested that there was a contingent of Confederate women from Strasburg who came to the battlefield after Early's morning successes and stripped the Union dead and brutalized some of the wounded Union soldiers. An Iowa soldier in the Army of the Shenandoah wrote after the battle that after Early's initial success, "Many of the women from Strausburg [*sic*] followed the army for the purpose of pillaging. Our wounded were subject to all manner of insults from these fiends."[247]

Sheridan's infantry pursued to the banks of Cedar Creek and stopped, while Union cavalry followed their counterparts toward Fisher's Hill. As the Union soldiers returned to the camps, which had been the scene of the morning's disaster, the veterans reflected on the day's events. Some Union soldiers focused on how Sheridan had kept his promise of the men returning to their old camps by nightfall. The chaplain of the 121st New York, Reverend John Adams, wrote after the battle, "True to General Sheridan's promise, we came back to our camp, which we left in the morning, and before eight at night it was announced to us officially that we had recaptured all we had lost."[248] Another veteran of the battle remarked, "Sheridan's promise was fulfilled, for we had our old camps as the evening fell."[249]

Others in the Army of the Shenandoah reflected on Sheridan's generalship and commended him for doing what was rarely done during any conflict—grasping victory from the depths of defeat. "History must give General Sheridan credit for doing what only such Generals as Napoleon and his kind have been able to do," explained the Twenty-ninth Maine's John Mead Gould. "To turn that army about and order a forward march without the help of a single fresh troop is wonderful…to halt…a huge mass of stragglers can only be done by those that are born with the wonderful gift."[250] The Nineteenth Corps' Colonel Edward Molineux, who particularly did not like Sheridan, set aside his personal dislike and reveled in Sheridan's ability to do the unthinkable at Cedar Creek. "Little as I like General Sheridan personally," Molineux explained to his sister, "I cannot but admire his firmness and ability, the fortunes of the day which commenced so disastrously for us, turned into a splendid victory."[251]

Despite the feelings of joy and adulation among the Union army, all of Sheridan's soldiers also realized the success came with a tremendous cost in human life. Regarded by a soldier in the Twenty-second Iowa as "the hardest battle [he] ever saw fought," casualties on both sides were high.[252] Early suffered approximately 3,100 casualties, about 1,200 of whom were captured during the Union assault. Additionally, Early lost twenty-four artillery pieces, numerous battle standards and wagons. Sheridan's Army of the Shenandoah lost nearly 5,800 men in the battle, the majority of whom were wounded, missing or captured, and 569 of whom were killed.[253] Amid the celebrations of Union victory came the grisly task of burying the dead and caring for the wounded. When Colonel Molinuex returned to where his headquarters had been in the morning, he saw what appeared to be a "perfect slaughter house filled with killed and wounded, dead horses and shell and shot."[254] Cedar Creek was bittersweet when the survivors of the Army of the Shenandoah bedded down after the battle. Although the victory had been achieved, it came at the sacrifice of human life—the lives of friends and brothers. "Among our camps," recalled the surgeon of the Seventy-seventh New York on the night of October 19, "the spades of the pioneers were heard as they hollowed out the shallow graves; and as we threw ourselves upon the ground to rest, we mourned for our comrades, and we rejoiced for our victory."[255]

As the battle's slaughter covered the landscape, some area civilians came to the battlefield to see what assistance they might offer to the suffering soldiers of both sides. Although some of these civilians held Confederate sympathies, in the aftermath of battle their allegiance took a secondary place to their humanity. "Mercy abandons the arena of battle," observed Colonel Keifer, "but when the conflict is ended *mercy* again asserts itself."[256] Among the locals to visit the battlefield was a member of the Shull family. After the war, Annie Shull recalled that after the battle ended, her "mother went to the battlefield to care for the wounded and said it was the worst sight she ever saw, men, and mules and horses lay thick on the ground." Shull even believed that some of the Union soldiers she encountered had actually taken property from her prior to the battle, but still she seemed to put aside her differences and aid those who clung desperately to life. "She saw some that robbed us…before," Shull remembered, "and did all she could for all, not many rebels among them."[257]

Regardless of local civilians' efforts to help the wounded soldiers, Union doctors in the battle's aftermath still confronted a tremendous burden in caring for the wounded. Area buildings were occupied as makeshift hospitals. St. Thomas Episcopal Church transformed from a house of worship into a hospital, and the Stickleys' home, which had been utilized by Confederate surgeons during the battle's opening phase, had now been commandeered by Union doctors. The scene inside the Stickleys' brick home was horrific. Mary Stickley recalled after the war that Union surgeons utilized the back porch for amputations and that the blood was so thick on the porch that her father had to clear "the blood off with a shovel."[258] Soldiers stable enough to be transported were sent north to Winchester, where a massive field hospital had been established after the Third Battle of Winchester. Union doctors earned the praise of many for their handling of the situation after Cedar Creek. "To an efficient medical corps," Colonel Keifer penned, "belongs the chief credit for the good work done in caring for the unfortunate."[259]

Although doctors tried their best to save the wounded of both sides, efforts at times proved futile, and the number of temporary graves on the

General George Crook. *Battles and Leaders*.

battlefield increased in the days after the battle. One resident of Middletown remembered that after the battle, some of the dead soldiers were put in simple pine coffins and stacked against the back wall of St. Thomas Episcopal Church. Some of the coffins remained outdoors for nearly a month before burial or being sent home. The Middletown native, whose macabre curiosity about the condition of these deceased soldiers got the better of him, wrote, "I pried open a number of 'em and looked in. Some of the dead men was very natural and other wasn't fit to look at. One man with a blanket wrapped about him was petrified, and his appearance hadn't changed any since he was buried, only his hair had growed way down, and his beard had growed long."[260] Each day the number of graves on the battlefield increased. Mary Stickley recalled that a "good many of the dead were buried on our place."[261] Colonel Molineux lamented of the sad scene, "Burying parties are at work…How sad to see the whole ground dotted with graves."[262]

While Union soldiers reveled in their success and confronted the battle's grisly aftermath, their Confederate counterparts also took stock of the day's fighting. From General Early's perspective, the bulk of his army had behaved cowardly during the afternoon. "This was the case of a glorious victory given up by my own troops after they had won it," Early concluded after the war.[263] When Early informed Lee of his loss at Cedar Creek, he confessed to his superior that to attempt an explanation as to the cause of the defeat was "mortifying." Early placed none of the blame for the defeat on his shoulders. Instead, Early explained to Lee that the reversal of fortunes at Cedar Creek "are due to no want of effort on my part."[264] Although some former Confederates, such as General Gordon, lambasted Early for his failure to pursue the Army of the Shenandoah in the morning and his unwillingness to send additional infantry support to bolster the army's left flank, many Confederates—both in the immediate aftermath of Cedar Creek and in the postwar years—defended Early's conduct. One Confederate soldier wrote two days after the battle that Cedar Creek "was a victory and a defeat. Early should be credited with the former—not charged with the latter. God knows I pull for and sympathize with him."[265] The Thirteenth Virginia's Captain Samuel Buck echoed his support for Early: "Gen. Early deserved great credit for this battle; won a victory second to none in the war and lost all by no fault of his own. He deserved a better fate." Buck, who published his reminiscences of the Civil War in 1925, believed that Gordon's observations and those of his supporters were unnecessarily abusive to Early's legacy. "Some of Gen. Gordon's admirers claim he planned the battle and would have won the victory had Gen. Early not come upon the field. I do not believe a word of it."[266]

Where Confederate soldiers placed blame, Sheridan's men counted their blessings. As celebrations took place on the grounds in front of his headquarters at Belle Grove, Sheridan sat down and went over the day's saga with his old friend General Crook. During the course of the conversation, Sheridan informed Crook, "I am going to get much more credit for this than I deserve."[267] Sheridan could have never imagined on the night of October 19, 1864, as he reflected on the battle, how significant his most recent success in the Shenandoah would become and how this battle—more than any other in Sheridan's illustrious military career—would define his military legacy and place him among the pantheon of our nation's greatest military commanders.

Chapter 5

"The thanks of the nation"

In the immediate days that followed the Union victory at Cedar Creek, news spread rapidly of Sheridan's successes. When members of President Lincoln's cabinet heard the news, they were tremendously pleased with another victory in the Valley. Secretary of State William Seward remarked in his diary, "The marked military event of the last week was the battle of Cedar Creek."[268] No one, however, could have been more pleased to learn of Sheridan's triumph than President Lincoln. Upon hearing the news, Lincoln sent Sheridan a short congratulatory note. "With great pleasure I tender to you and your brave army the thanks of the nation," Lincoln wrote Sheridan, "and my own personal admiration and gratitude for the month's operations in the Shenandoah Valley; and especially for the splendid work of October 19, 1864."[269] Aside from the battle's military results—essentially wresting the Valley from Confederate hands, thus guaranteeing Washington's safety from a Confederate attack and preventing the Valley's use as a source of provender for Confederate forces operating elsewhere in Virginia—Cedar Creek came at a most opportune moment in Lincoln's political life.

As the 1864 presidential election neared, Lincoln did not feel especially confident that he would win reelection and defeat the Democratic candidate—former Union General George B. McClellan. Sheridan's successes in the Valley, coupled with equal achievements of General William T. Sherman in Georgia that autumn, bolstered Lincoln's political stability. Against the backdrop of Sheridan's success at Cedar Creek, Republicans in Washington, D.C., buzzed with optimism for Lincoln's chances of reelection. On the evening of October 21, Lincoln supporters held a torchlight parade, where they cheered Sheridan and defamed McClellan's image at the same time. Some Republican supporters from New Jersey carried a large portrait of McClellan in the parade with the words "Great Failure of the War" emblazoned across it.[270] The torchlight parade concluded in front of the Executive Mansion, where a large crowd gathered and cheered for Lincoln. They demanded that the president make a few appropriate remarks. Lincoln had not prepared an address, but he did tell his supporters that they should not necessarily be cheering for him, but rather for the Union general who raised the Republicans' mood. "I was promised not to be called upon for a speech to-night, nor do I propose to make one. But, as we have been hearing some very good news for a day or two," Lincoln told the audience, "I propose that you give three hearty cheers for Sheridan." Lincoln continued in praise of Sheridan, "While we are at it we may as well consider how fortunate it was for the Secesh that Sheridan was a very little man. If he had been a large man, there is no knowing what he would have done with them." As Lincoln closed his impromptu speech, he also asked those in attendance to praise General Grant, who changed the Valley's strategic vision by appointing Sheridan to command. "I propose three cheers for General Grant," Lincoln remarked, "who knew to what use to put Sheridan; three cheers for all our noble commanders and the soldiers and sailors; three cheers for all people everywhere who cheer the soldiers and sailors of the Union—and now, good night."[271]

In addition to political rallies in the nation's capital inspired by Sheridan's successes, people in Washington witnessed firsthand Union soldiers bringing the trophies of their victory for presentation to the War Department in the days following Cedar Creek. For example, on October 23, General Custer arrived in Washington to present captured battle flags to Secretary Stanton. Custer entered the nation's capital amid fanfare. The flamboyant cavalier placed ten of the enemy's captured flags on his locomotive as it steamed into the nation's capital. Among the standards presented to the secretary of war was the headquarters flag of General Ramseur. Additionally, Custer presented Stanton with Confederate cannons, which, after being unloaded from the train, were driven in a triumphal parade, led by a brass band, to the War Department.[272]

With the various military successes in the autumn of 1864, Lincoln ably mustered enough political support to defeat McClellan. Lincoln won a majority of the popular vote in 1864, including 78 percent of the votes from Union soldiers in the field—a segment of the electorate that McClellan hoped to capture.[273] With his political success secured, Lincoln showed his appreciation to those military commanders who had played a vital role in prolonging his presidency. On November 14, 1864, Lincoln issued General

Orders No. 282, which announced Sheridan's promotion to major general in the regular army. Lincoln specifically cited Sheridan's victory at Cedar Creek as the justification for the promotion. "That for the personal gallantry, military skill, and just confidence in the courage and patriotism of his troops, displayed by Philip H. Sheridan, on the 19th day of October, at Cedar Run [Creek], whereby, under the blessing of Providence," Lincoln explained in the order, "his routed army was reorganized, a great national disaster averted, and a brilliant victory achieved over the rebels for the third time in pitched battle within thirty days, Philip H. Sheridan is appointed Major-General in the U.S. Army."[274]

While Lincoln and fellow Republicans heaped adulation and praise upon Sheridan in Cedar Creek's wake, the entire nation soon began to learn about Cedar Creek and Sheridan's conduct through newspaper accounts, which earned Sheridan the country's admiration. Some newspapers reported that the victory at Cedar Creek solidified the high spirits of the Army of the Shenandoah and effectively ended any Confederate hopes of holding onto the Shenandoah Valley. The *New York Evening Post* reported on October 25, "The enthusiasm of our men after the defeat of the enemy is described by General Custer as magnificent, and their confidence in Sheridan is so great… It is generally believed by our officers that there will be no more serious fighting in the Valley, it being impossible for the Richmond authorities to reinforce Early's wasted columns now scattered along the lines of retreat."[275] The *New York Tribune* echoed that Cedar Creek "was the most thorough defeat of Early which he has yet received from the hands of Sheridan. The fortunes of the day were more than retrieved."[276] Other newspapers even reportedly interviewed Confederate prisoners of war at Harpers Ferry who had been captured at Cedar Creek, who told Northern reporters "that Sheridan is the best General against whom they have ever fought and that his dashing tactics are more than a match for even Jubal Early."[277]

Although most newspapers focused on the facts of the battle and wanted to convey the mood among the Army of the Shenandoah and of Early's battered command, some of the Northern press decided to use more elaborate language and focus on one event of the battle to convey a sense of Sheridan's generalship—his ride from Winchester. On October 24, 1864, the *New York Herald* cited Sheridan's ride and subsequent arrival as the pivotal moment in the engagement. "He came into action with a small escort," the *Herald* reported, "and his horse in a heavy perspiration, having come on a dead run…his presence was known, the troops made the air reverberate with cheers."[278] Less than two weeks after the *Herald*'s account of Sheridan's arrival, *Harper's Weekly* utilized the story of Sheridan's ride as the cover story. A full front-page image of Sheridan astride Rienzi sketched by Sol Eytings graced the cover. "It was a victory following upon the heels of apparent reverse," *Harper's* reported, "and therefore reflecting peculiar credit on the brave commander to whose timely arrival upon the field the final success of the day must be attributed." The reporter for *Harper's Weekly* also asserted that "Sheridan's ride to the front, will go down in history as one of the most important and exciting events which have ever given interest to a battle scene, and to this event will be attributed the victory of the day." Even General Grant praised Sheridan for this remarkable feat. Sheridan turned, in Grant's estimation, "what bid fair to be a disaster into a glorious victory," and in Grant's view this made "Sheridan what I have always thought of him, one of the ablest Generals."[279]

Despite the coverage the Northern press gave to Sheridan and his ride from Winchester, perhaps nothing solidified Sheridan's place in the collective consciousness of American society more than Thomas Buchanan Read's epic poem "Sheridan's Ride." According to some accounts, the influence for Read to pen the famous stanzas came when he read the story about the event from *Harper's Weekly*; however, that is unlikely, as *Harper's* ran its story of Sheridan at Cedar Creek on November 5, 1864, and the first performance of Read's poem occurred on October 31, 1864. Another account associated with *Harper's*, obviously incorrect, stated that, on the morning of October 31, Read got up late and lounged around the home of Cryus Garrett—Read's brother-in-law—in Cincinnati, Ohio. Garrett, apparently aggravated at Read's laziness, slammed a copy of *Harper's Weekly* in his lap. "There… see what you missed," Garrett informed Read, "you ought to have drawn that picture yourself…the first thing you know somebody will write a poem on that event, and you will be beaten all around." According to this version, Read went upstairs and in several hours penned the famous lines.[280]

Other accounts state that Read's close friend, Shakespearean actor Thomas Murdoch, became the catalyst for the poem. Following the news of Cedar Creek, both Read and Murdoch were in Cincinnati, Ohio. At the time Read lived there, and Murdoch was in town to receive the congratulation of its citizens for playing such an integral role in raising funds for the United States Sanitary Commission. One source indicated that during a late afternoon at the end of October, Read and Murdoch strolled down a Cincinnati street, drunk, when they encountered a newspaper with the story of the ride. Murdoch turned to Read and said that this would be perfect for a poem. Murdoch told Read that he would like to read the poem during the reception in his honor at Pike's Opera House. Read, according to this account, agreed, went to a local tavern and, in less than an hour's time, completed the poem.[281]

Discrepancies aside as to the inspiration for Read's famous words, they became public on the night of October 31 at Pike's Opera House as Murdoch read it to an enthusiastic crowd. A member of the audience noted how the poem energized the attendees: "The poem, a ringing, thrilling, dramatic production, was then recited, as only Mr. Murdoch could recite it. Each line picturing the fiery gallop of the fiery Sheridan, won the audience more and more, until it could no longer contain itself, and burst into a rapturous applause."[282] After Murdoch finished his recitation of Read's poem, the crowd erupted into cheers for him, Read and Sheridan. "Cheer after cheer went up from the great concourse that shook the building to its very foundation. Ladies waved their handkerchiefs and men their hats," recalled Murdoch of the audience's reaction.[283]

In the days after Murdoch's reading, newspapers across the North published "Sheridan's Ride." Republican politicians also reacted favorably to Read's poem and believed it could actually prove useful in Lincoln's bid for reelection. On Election Day, the *New York Tribune*, which feverishly supported Lincoln's campaign, printed Read's poem on the front page. Undoubtedly, the newspaper's editors believed that Read's poem would serve as a gentle reminder to voters of Sheridan's great victory and subsequently of Lincoln's ability as commander in chief.[284]

The rapid and widespread publication of "Sheridan's Ride" not only catapulted Sheridan's fame, but it also turned the horse that carried Sheridan to the battlefield—Rienzi—into a national hero. In his poem Read gave a tremendous amount of agency to Rienzi as he bore his master to the battlefield, fully cognizant of the immediacy of the situation. Read penned in his poem,

By the flash of his eye, and his red nostrils' play,
He seemed to the whole great army to say,
"I have brought you Sheridan all the way from Winchester down to save the day."

So popular had Rienzi become that some opportunistic individuals in the postwar years touted to have displays of this famous steed. For example, in 1876 P.T. Barnum had a traveling exhibit and collected fair amounts of money showing the bones of the famous war horse. What most people did

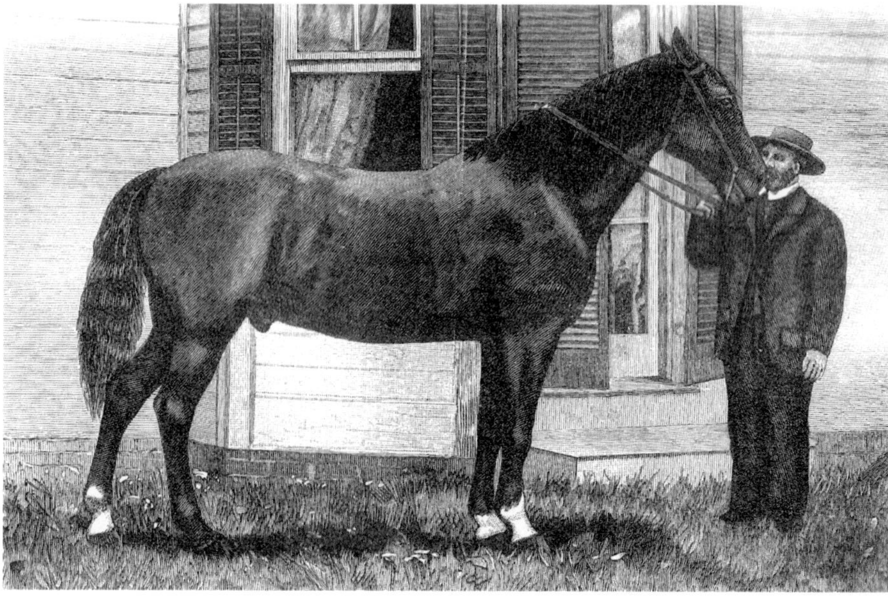

Rienzi, Sheridan's war horse, was renamed Winchester after Cedar Creek. *Personal Memoirs of P.H. Sheridan.*

not realize was that in 1876, Rienzi—officially renamed "Winchester" by Sheridan after Cedar Creek—was still alive. When reporters investigated the validity of Barnum's exhibit, a member of General Sheridan's staff informed them that the horse was still alive and with Sheridan in Chicago. Additionally, the officer informed the press that when Winchester did die, Sheridan would never subject his beloved horse's remains to this type of disrespectful display.[285] Two years later, in 1878, Sheridan's famous war horse passed away. Initially Sheridan had his steed mounted and presented its remains to the Governor's Island Military Museum in New York Harbor. In 1922 fire destroyed the museum, but the horse's remains survived. Officials from the museum turned the stuffed horse over to the Smithsonian Institution shortly after the fire, and that is where this famous mount continues to reside until this day.[286]

In the Civil War's aftermath, the event of Sheridan's Ride became one of the most popularly depicted pieces in painting—with only scenes of the Battle of Gettysburg and the battle between the ironclads USS *Monitor* and CSS *Virginia* being more popular subjects.[287] Aside from sketches that appeared in newspapers, the first major painting came from the skilled hand of the poet-artist Read. In the immediate months following the conflict's conclusion, Read, who also had tremendous skill as a painter and sculptor, was approached by the Union League of Philadelphia to create an oil painting based on his famous poem. Read wanted the painting to be as historically accurate as possible, and so he spent several weeks with Sheridan and his war horse in New Orleans, where he sketched and made detailed studies of his subjects.[288]

When Read unveiled the painting at an exhibition at the Philadelphia Academy of Fine Arts in March 1870, it became, as had been the case with his poem, a sensation. Over the first month the painting sat on display, more than thirty thousand visitors came to view it.[289] All who viewed it seemed awestruck. "The flashing eye; the close-cut military style of the hair; the fierce moustache; the row of three buttons marking exalted grade; the vigorous yet graceful movement of the sword arm, and the cap disappearing in the distance," recalled a visitor to the exhibition, "indicative of the remarkable time making…all of these are admirable points in the picture…and worthy of being closely studied by the student of Art."[290] Understandably the visitors with the most critical eye to Read's painting were the men who had served with Sheridan in the Valley. They too enjoyed this depiction of their revered general. Captain Laurence Kip had been so moved by the painting's clarity and realism that he sent Read a congratulatory note. "Allow me to express my great satisfaction," Kip explained to Read. "I consider it a most excellent likeness of my late Chief, and a faithful representation of his favorite horse. You have expressed on canvass all the life and fire he displayed upon the day he took his celebrated ride, when he turned defeat into victory."[291]

With the popularity and success of Read's painting, other artists over the succeeding decades attempted to capture the event in their own artistic style. In 1886 Louis Prang published Thur de Thulstrup's version of the event as a chromo lithograph. Sheridan did not necessarily approve of this version of the event, stating that he did not carry a flag in one hand and wave the other and that the painting made him appear to be a "fool." However, it became a popular item and many households throughout the North purchased it to decorate their homes.[292] Nearly four years later, Charles H. Andrus, an artist from Vermont, unveiled his version of the historic events of Cedar Creek. Unlike Thulstrup's depiction, Andrus wanted to portray the event as accurately as possible. Andrus believed that his massive painting, which occupied 472 square feet, was the most correct portrayal of the event to date. No "artist has yet depicted upon canvas a painting worthy of this grand subject," Andrus asserted.[293]

Photogravure of Thomas Buchanan Read's *Sheridan's Ride. Author's collection.*

Prang chromolithograph of *Sheridan's Ride*. *Library of Congress.*

As the fame of the event increased along with Sheridan's legend all types of individuals wanted to draw upon the recognition of Sheridan and Cedar Creek to sell items of all types. The First National Bank of Yarmouth, Massachusetts, utilized an image of Sheridan rallying his army to advertise its services of "General Banking, Safe Deposit Boxes, and Administration and Trusteeship of Estates," while the Boston Mutual Life Insurance Company used the event for an advertisement.[294]

Book publishers also drew on the popularity of the event to entice readers to buy their books. In 1897 T.C. DeLeon published his book *Crag-Nest: A Romance of the Day's of Sheridan's Ride*, a novel about a Shenandoah Valley family during the conflict. Regardless of the author's use of the event as a marketing tool, DeLeon took great pains in the book's opening pages to condemn how this one episode had been exaggerated by authors and artists falsely elevating Sheridan to the pantheon of great American generals. The Alabama author stated that Sheridan's ride was nothing more than an "everyday affair—equally from the strategist's and the horseman's view; not even an excuse for enthusiasts to hang paeans upon."[295]

While DeLeon referred to the ride as an "everyday affair," some looked upon the ride with skepticism, and they doubted the story's validity, feeling it had been embellished so much in the conflict's aftermath that the truth of it was lost. What caused some to doubt the event's validity had been Read's poem. In order to construct the poem, Read stated that Sheridan had been in Winchester—twenty miles away—when he set out for his army. Although the distance from Winchester to his army was about a dozen miles, Read took literary license in order for the poem to rhyme and make sense from an artistic perspective, not a military one. A number of bitter Confederate veterans used this as ammunition to attack Sheridan's reputation in the postwar era. One Confederate veteran wrote in 1923 that "the Myth of Sheridan's Ride galloped to meet his fleeing army near Middletown, about seven or eight [also incorrect], *and not twenty*, miles from Winchester."[296] Another veteran of Early's army wrote after the conflict, "History leaves no room to doubt that he actually rode from Winchester to Middletown… [however] all the glamour, glory and renown with which Read's poetical effusion emblazons this ride, are just about as fictitious and mythical as the existence of, and the many glorious attributes given to Barbara Fritchie, as portrayed by Whittier's poem."[297]

Some of Sheridan's veterans came to Little Phil's defense in the postwar years as the legacy of his ride came under scrutiny. The Twenty-ninth Maine's John Mead Gould, who penned the regiment's history five years after the war, believed that what Read wrote should not detract from Sheridan's memory. Gould simply observed, "Poetic license permits Buchanan Read to

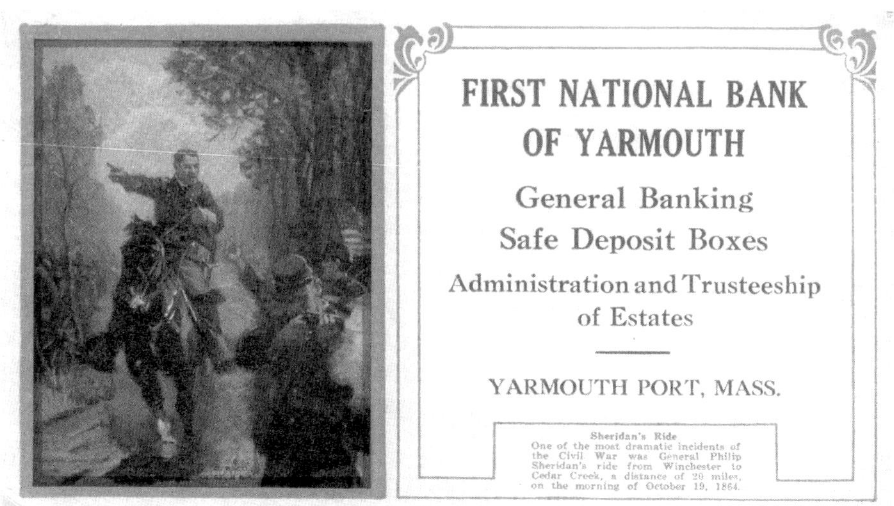

Yarmouth Bank Advertisement utilizing the popularity of Sheridan's Ride. *Author's collection.*

state that Sheridan was twenty miles away, for that best of reasons, that the word twenty sounds much better than fifteen."[298]

Despite the manner in which some attacked Sheridan's ride, the event, especially for many in the North, became inspirational—a study in courage, heroism and patriotism. Various textbooks and general history books published in the immediate decades following the war's end utilized the ride as a moment to teach the nation's youth about heroes. For example, when Thomas Wentworth Higginson published his *Young Folks' History of the United States*, in 1887, he used the events of Sheridan's arrival at Cedar Creek as depicted in Read's poem to inspire the country's young students. "Sheridan had news of the fight when at Winchester, twenty miles away, and rode that distance at furious speed…Meeting his retreating troops, he rallied them and turned defeat into victory," Higginson explained.[299]

Additionally, some veterans of the Army of the Shenandoah's campaigns believed that Sheridan's ride should be a story passed down from one generation to the next. One veteran of the campaign—Russell Hastings, who had been wounded at Third Winchester and therefore did not participate in Cedar Creek—noted that he would advise all future generations in his family to read it. "Buchanan Read has written a poem on the coming up of Sheridan from Winchester twenty miles away," Hastings penned in his unpublished memoirs. "I advise all my descendants to read it."[300]

By the time of General Sheridan's death in August 1888, his ride to his army at Cedar Creek emerged as his popular defining moment. While the nation mourned the passing of a great national hero, all of the orations and memorials in Sheridan's honor seemed to focus on one episode of his life—Cedar Creek. When the State of New York held a memorial in Sheridan's honor, many of those who delivered eulogies looked back to October 19, 1864, as the day that defined Sheridan. "At Cedar Creek his army was already routed, when his famous ride brought him upon the field," stated one of the New York orations. "His coming on the field at Cedar Creek after his ride from Winchester has often been regarded as a species of apocalypse."[301] When the City of Boston held its ceremony, speeches in Sheridan's honor also focused on Cedar Creek. One of the orators, identified as a Mr. Sullivan, believed that with his handling of the situation at Cedar Creek Sheridan "became the sublime hero of the Shenandoah Valley, so much so, that when the name of Sheridan was heard in the valley from the day when he rode twenty miles away and saved the Union army from defeat…Sheridan was indeed a sublime soldier."[302]

Albumen photograph of General Sheridan's grave monument in Arlington National Cemetery. *Author's collection.*

Even during Sheridan's funeral mass, held at St. Matthew's in Washington, D.C., his conduct at Cedar Creek became the focal point of remembrance. When Cardinal Gibbon, who presided over the Catholic funeral rite, delivered the eulogy for General Sheridan he seemed to fixate on Cedar Creek as the defining moment of Sheridan's life. "I have neither the time nor the ability to dwell upon his military career from the time he left West Point till the close of the war," Gibbon stated, "[so] let me select one incident which reveals to us his quickness of conception and readiness of execution. I refer to his famous ride in the Valley of Virginia." As Gibbon attempted to reconstruct the scene he certainly relied heavily on the image of Sheridan as portrayed by Thomas Buchanan Read. "As he is advancing along the road he sees his routed army rushing pell-mell toward him. Quick as thought—by the glance of his eye," Gibbon told the mourners, "by the power of his word, by the strength of his will—he hurls back that living stream on the enemy and snatches victory from the jaws of defeat."[303]

Clearly by the time of Sheridan's death and for decades afterward, his handling of the situation at Cedar Creek emerged as his defining moment. Perhaps a veteran of Sheridan's campaign in the Valley best captured what Sheridan meant to victory at Cedar Creek and what the battle meant to his legacy. During a reunion of the Eighth Vermont and First Vermont Cavalry held in Montpelier, Vermont, Colonel Herbert E. Hill succinctly captured the battle's significance to Sheridan's legacy: "Sheridan showed consummate generalship here, for he plucked glory from calamity: his crown was Cedar Creek."[304]

Chapter 6

"They come not with fire and sword"

During a postwar reunion of Vermonters in Montpelier who served in Sheridan's 1864 Shenandoah Campaign, the Eighth Vermont's Colonel Herbert E. Hill addressed the gathering and reflected on their involvement in the campaign. "The campaign was a notable one," Hill stated, "no campaign during the four years of bloody war attracted more attention, none saw fiercer fighting or more decisive results…The battle of Cedar Creek stands out like a lone sentinel, totally unlike any other battle of the war. In one brief day the veteran was plunged in the fathomless depths of crushing defeat, and then as suddenly lifted to the dizzy heights of glorious victory."[305] For veterans of Sheridan's army the Battle of Cedar Creek helped to define their military legacy. Because it established their reputation as soldiers, the veterans eagerly wanted to visit that battlefield and all those of Sheridan's campaign. Unfortunately, for nearly twenty years after the conflict's end, a visit of Sheridan's veterans to the Valley's battlefields proved an impossible task.

Not only had postwar Reconstruction emerged as an obstacle to Sheridan's veterans—or for that matter other Union veterans who desired to visit other parts of the South to commemorate their service—but many former Confederates in the Valley also harbored intense animosity toward Sheridan and the Army of the Shenandoah. Little Phil's army became the focus of hatred, as it was during his army's tenure in the Valley that the most widespread destruction of private property occurred in such a short period of time—"The Burning." Many Valley residents placed all of the blame for problems confronted by the region's inhabitants in the war's aftermath squarely on the Army of the Shenandoah's shoulders. "Poverty stared the citizens in the face, as this was in the fall season of the year, and too late to raise any provisions. Their horses and cattle were all gone," a Valley native wrote of the impact of Sheridan's operations, "their farm implements burnt and no prospects of producing anything next year."[306]

However, once military Reconstruction ended across the South with the Compromise of 1877—coupled with an increased stability in the Shenandoah Valley's economy as crop outputs rose to prewar levels along with population recovery—many Valley residents and former Confederates began to accept the war's results.[307] Visitors to the Valley by the 1880s noted how the war's scars seemed to be less visible. "Where then was seen on every hand the black cinders of war the traveler now finds all the arts and industries of peace," noted a Northern visitor in 1885. "He finds a rich agricultural region that will compare favorably with any east of the Alleghenies. And in place of the desolate haunts of twenty years ago he find a rapidly increasing, prosperous population, with well-filled barns and storehouses and with happy firesides."[308] In addition to recovery, Union veterans and Northerners in general began to not just view the South as an old battleground, but rather as a place for vacation and relaxation. "They have a valley rich and fertile and are gradually recovering what they lost," observed a tourist to the Valley in the 1880s. "Instead of a battle field the Valley of Virginia has been changed to an immense summer resort. Numerous springs and summer hotels dot the mountain sides and there is no more imposing mountain scenery anywhere."[309]

As postwar reconciliation emerged, by the early 1880s veterans of Sheridan's campaign in the Valley seized the opportunity to visit the battlefields of the 1864 Shenandoah Campaign. Under direction of the Fourteenth New Hampshire's Colonel Carroll Wright, the Sheridan's Veterans Association formed in the autumn of 1882 to organize a visit to the Shenandoah Valley and visit the battlefields where nearly twenty thousand soldiers of both blue and gray became casualties in the Valley's bloodiest campaign. The association worked diligently to plan a visit that coincided with the nineteenth anniversary of the campaign. The veterans realized that this visit to the Valley provided "the opportunity of a lifetime for the veterans who followed Sheridan to victory, to revisit the scenes of their triumphs, to contrast the dreadful past with the happy present and experience the sincere and royal welcome which generous Southern hearts could extend to former foes."[310]

Colonel Carroll D. Wright, president of the Sheridan's Veterans Association. *Sheridan's Veterans, 1883*.

Remarkably, to the veterans' astonishment, a seemingly large majority of Valley residents welcomed the veterans with open arms. A Charles Town, West Virginia newspaper noted that the citizens of Winchester greeted the more than two hundred members of the Sheridan's Veterans Association with "distinguished honors."[311] During this first visit in the Valley, the veterans of the Army of the Shenandoah informed their former Confederate counterparts that they had not come as conquerors to gloat about their successes, but rather to honor the heroism of soldiers. "We do come as soldiers, to meet the brave men who withstood us manfully in battle," Colonel Wright informed Valley inhabitants during his welcoming address, "and to pay the tribute which the valor of Confederate troops has ever won from the soldiers of the Federal army. The war testified to the world the valor of American arms, and this is all we wish to carry in our memories. Brave men fought brave men, fighting for the principle they believed to be sacred, and out of this fighting has come the American soldier."[312]

Throughout their week in the Valley, the veterans held ceremonies in the Winchester National Cemetery, laid flowers on Confederate graves in Winchester's Stonewall Cemetery and visited the campaign's battlefields. On September 22, 1883, the veterans journeyed to Cedar Creek. They first visited the site of Sheridan's old headquarters—Belle Grove. The property's owner—James Smellie—welcomed the veterans with open arms. After they ate lunch at Belle Grove they then scattered in all directions to visit the sites where their regiments fought. When the veterans searched for old battle lines and camps they noted that the landscape had changed little from when they fought there in 1864. "The topography has changed but little," recalled a Nineteenth Corps' veteran, "and there was no difficulty in finding

Reunion ribbon worn by veterans of the Nineteenth Corps during their visit to the Valley and Cedar Creek in 1883. *Author's collection.*

the sites of the old camps, the temporary breastworks thrown up in places, and also so many souvenirs and relics of the fight."[313] The veterans had only several hours to visit Cedar Creek, and before the veterans departed the field, they determined that another visit to the Valley had to be made at a later date to allow a proper amount of time for reflection and remembrance on the campaign's most significant battlefield. One veteran observed, "It was already apparent that the time included within the limits of the excursion was altogether too short for any thorough exploration of the battlefields, and it was generally conceded that another visit to the Valley must be made within a few years. The wonderful field of Cedar Creek was not satisfactorily traversed by the veterans."[314]

The veterans reflected positively on their experience in 1883, and likewise, most Valley inhabitants exhibited positive sentiment as to how the visits by Sheridan's veterans would help to cement the bond of reconciliation. "The behavior of the excursionists is highly extolled by all," reported a Valley newspaper, "and it is to be hoped that the visit will go far toward exciting friendly feelings between the two sections of the country."[315]

Sheridan's veterans came back to the Valley two years later, and on September 21, 1885, the veterans returned to Cedar Creek. Among the activities planned for the Cedar Creek commemoration was a recreation of Sheridan's famed ride. Eleven members of the association rented horses in Winchester and rode the path that Sheridan took as he made his way to his army at Cedar Creek. "One of the novel episodes of the trip to Cedar Creek was the horseback party which went over the identical ground of Sheridan's Ride," recalled the Fourteenth New Hampshire's Francis Buffum, who was among eleven men to recreate the ride, "starting from the very house where Little Phil mounted, on that fateful morning, and continuing over the General's course to the point where he rallied his troops

Veterans of Sheridan's army gather on the steps of Belle Grove in 1883. *United States Army Military History Institute.*

to their magnificent victory."[316] Unlike Sheridan, the men did not make a gallant dash for Middletown; however, as Buffum recalled: "It was a jolly ride, and some of the valiant knights got left—behind."[317]

After the veterans arrived at Cedar Creek, they turned their attention to a monument dedication to honor the Eighth Vermont. The Vermonters chose the ridge that they defended on the east side of the Valley Pike during the battle's morning phase as the spot to immortalize their role in the morning's action. The monument contained no fanciful carvings or bronze soldiers, but rather was a simple block of Vermont marble. Veterans of the Eighth Vermont believed that this simple heavy stone ably memorialized the actions of their regiment. "In design it is most appropriate—a massive block of marble," recalled one veteran, "standing on the ground without base or adjunct of any kind, rough on three sides but smoothed on the fourth for the inscription."[318] During the dedicatory remarks of Colonel Herbert E. Hill—which were delivered before not only Union veterans, but veterans of the Confederate army as well who fought on that field—he stated that the simple design of the monument had tremendous symbolic importance. The monument, Hill commented, "was purposely carved and fashioned on three sides in rough, to represent the savage and peculiar features of that awful struggle." The monument's three rough sides represented how the regiment at one point was surrounded on three sides and additionally signified the regiment's three color bearers "who were shot down in the terrible hand-to-hand conflict and who died."[319] Lastly the three unfinished sides of the monument symbolized the nearly three-fourths casualties that the regiment suffered during the battle.[320]

In addition to the monument's highly emblematic importance, it also stood as a testament to reconciliation in the Valley. The Eighth Vermont's Captain S.E. Howard, who had been wounded on the spot where the monument was dedicated, believed that the monument also stood as a pillar of fraternity among former enemies. Howard told the crowd of veterans from both armies that it had not been placed there "for glorification, but to mark the spot where our comrades fell, to mark the place of an important public event, and a turning point in a nation's history; let it also have a deeper meaning to us of the North and you our brothers in the South. Let it be a pillar stone which shall forever mark an era of genuine fraternal feeling between *us.* Let it be an everlasting covenant that we will not pass over this stone to thee, and thou shalt not pass over this pillar to us, for harm."[321]

Following the dedication, veterans of both armies strolled over the battlefield and reminisced. One member of the association noted how the passage of

Eighth Vermont monument at Cedar Creek, dedicated in 1885. *Photograph by author.*

twenty-one years had turned former enemies into comrades. Men who once shot at each other at Cedar Creek now walked over the battlefield "side by side, if not arm in arm…and these men who then thought of themselves enemies now meet as friends."[322] Members of the association, along with former Confederate veterans, fully understood that for the nation's longevity, they had to put aside old animosities to strengthen the American Republic. During the remarks delivered at the Eighth Vermont monument dedication, one of the orators urged the veterans of both blue and gray to "let loyalty and fraternity everywhere prevail, and all the social and moral virtues have a high rating with us as a people. Then will there be ground for the hope that the future of our beloved country may be worthy of its glorious past."[323]

Interactions and exchanges such as these on the Cedar Creek battlefield caught the attention of Southern politicians and Valley inhabitants alike. Among the politicians to approve of this fraternity among former enemies was former Confederate General Fitzhugh Lee, a veteran of the 1864 Shenandoah Campaign and a powerful figure in postwar Virginia politics. Approving of their visit to the Valley in 1885, Lee informed the veterans via letter that "such reunions result in producing a fraternal feeling among the sections and strengthening the union of States…the South is marching steadily forward and…she is not chanting miseries over a struggle of a quarter century ago, but is waving the star-spangled banner and hopes the 'bloody shirt' will be furled forever."[324] Likewise, some of the Valley's civilian population noticed how the veterans of the Army of the Shenandoah extended a hand of reconciliation. "They come not with fire and sword," noted a female in the Valley, "but with countenances beaming with peace and good will and the right hand of fellowship extended to express their willingness to be brothers again…The Southerner who can clasp that extended hand, without one resentful, revengeful feeling, should be called the 'Noblest Roman of them all.'"[325]

Following the Eighth Vermont's impressive and meaningful ceremonies the veterans of the Fourteenth New Hampshire visited an impromptu memorial—a pile of stones—they had placed there in 1883. Remarkably, they found their makeshift monument still intact and determined to mark the spot more permanently in the future, which unfortunately, for reasons unknown, has never been accomplished.

Throughout that September day, the Cedar Creek battlefield buzzed with activity. "Horseman are galloping from point to point;" recalled Francis Buffum of the scene, "an interested group is over inspecting the Vermont monument; veterans and ladies are roaming up and down the pike; Sixth Corps men are reconnoitering their old position; the Nineteenth Corps breastworks and the rolling plain are dotted with excursionists…far to the left front of the tragic lines of the Eighth Corps are being inspected."[326] After the veterans visited the sites on the battlefield, they once again gathered around Belle Grove, where the owner opened its doors for dinner. Following the meal the veterans departed Cedar Creek for Winchester. For many, this would be the last time that they ever set foot on that battlefield. The day's activities at Cedar Creek had served its roles of reflection, remembrance and reconciliation. One member of the party reflected simply of the visit to Cedar Creek, "It was one of the most profitable days of the excursion, and was thoroughly enjoyed."[327]

128th New York monument at Cedar Creek, dedicated in 1907. *Photograph by author.*

Following its reunion in the Valley in 1885, the Sheridan's Veterans Association would never return again to the Shenandoah as a collective to honor the Valley's past and further postwar reconciliation, although individual regimental associations returned there annually to honor their part in the campaign. Each time the veterans came to the Valley, they visited the fields and reflected on their involvement, but it would be some time before Union veterans erected another monument on the Cedar Creek battlefield.

In 1904 veterans of the 128th New York—a unit that served in General Emory's Nineteenth Corps—decided to raise a monument to the regiment on the Cedar Creek battlefield "to memorialize the men who lost their lives in that engagement."[328] Over approximately three years, the veterans raised money for the construction of the monument and purchase of a small parcel of land at the left end of the Nineteenth Corps' trench lines along the west side of the Valley Pike. The 128th Veterans Association contracted Henry P. Rieger of Baltimore to manufacture the granite monument.[329] Finally, on October 15, 1907, the New York veterans gathered on the Cedar Creek battlefield. A party of thirty-eight veterans arrived in Winchester on the evening of October 14 and the following day made their trek to Cedar Creek.

As had been the case in all prior visits to the Valley, the New Yorkers received a warm welcome, and when they arrived at Cedar Creek the members of Strasburg's Stover Camp of Confederate veterans greeted them and participated in the ceremonies. The former Confederates "were among the most interested spectators," recalled one of the New Yorkers, and assisted the guests however they could.[330]

During the opening remarks, veteran Derrick Brown gathered the spectators and told them, in rhetoric typical of reconciliation, that this monument not only marked the spot of the New Yorkers' heroic deeds in the epic battle of the 1864 Shenandoah Campaign, but that it also "marks the spot where men met men and Americans met Americans, all performing a duty required of them by that power and authority which each recognized as supreme in the sphere in which it acted for them and where were displayed those sterling traits of character that have made the American nation what it is today in the eyes of the whole civilized world." Additionally, as had become customary at many monument dedications throughout the South, Brown informed the Confederate veterans that this too served as a monument to their service and honored the legacy of those who fell at Cedar Creek for the Confederacy. "And so this stone will serve the specific purpose for which it has been erected," Brown stated, "and it will serve the broader and better purpose of memorializing every effort and every sacrifice made upon this soil, hallowed as it is by the blood here shed forty-three years ago."[331]

After the dedicatory remarks, a large American flag was pulled off and the monument unveiled. "This unveiling was the occasion of loud cheers, in which the Confederate veterans heartily joined," recalled one of the New Yorkers.[332] After the unveiling, Herbert S. Larrick—a lawyer from Winchester—addressed the crowd. Larrick informed the Union veterans that the memory of the Civil War and the South was very dear to them and that he, nor any former Confederate would apologize for the conflict, but that they were willing to put aside their differences in favor of national unity: "While we offer no apology for the position taken by the south on this great constitutional question, I believe that I voice the sentiments of a large majority of the southern people when I say that we would not have had that question decided other than it was. The memory of the old south is dear to us." Larrick reciprocated Brown's sentiments and stated that he admired the courage of the Union soldier in battle.[333]

Perhaps the most significant moment to the New Yorkers came when Larrick promised that Valley inhabitants would be good custodians of the 128th's monument. "If you would leave the monument into the custody of our people, you would find that we would guard it with the same tender care with which we guard those monuments which we have erected to the memory of our own dead." More importantly to reconciliation Larrick urged all those in attendance that they should not think of themselves as Northerners or Southerners, but rather as Americans. "Lastly," Larrick informed the crowd, "you should teach our young men that there is no north for the northerner, no south for the southerner, but one grand and glorious America for the patriotic and liberty-loving Americans."[334]

Monument erected in 1920 to honor General Stephen D. Ramseur. *Photograph by author.*

Thirteen years later, veterans of the blue and gray gathered on the Cedar Creek battlefield to dedicate a third and final monument—this time to the memory of General Stephen D. Ramseur. Erected under the auspices of the North Carolina Historical Commission and the North Carolina Division of the United Daughters of the Confederacy, a contingent of veterans from both sides gathered near the Belle Grove mansion on September 16, 1920, to dedicate the Ramseur monument.[335] Following the opening dedicatory remarks, two Confederate flags were pulled off the monument by General Ramseur's daughter, Mary. This must have been especially moving for Mary because she had never even met her father; at the time of his death, she was only several days old.[336]

Among the speakers that afternoon was Colonel Henry DuPont—a West Point classmate of Ramseur's and commander of artillery in General George Crook's Eighth Corps at Cedar Creek. For so many years, Confederate veterans participated in Union monument dedications, but actions such as DuPont's helped further heal the nation. DuPont did not identify Ramseur as his enemy at Cedar Creek, but rather as his longtime friend. "As a close friend of my youthful days, I held him in most affectionate remembrance, and as I happened to have been personally concerned in much, if not all, that occurred from the time he fell mortally wounded on the Cedar Creek battlefield, October 19, 1864, until the end came during the early hours of the following day, I was exceedingly desirous that the information in my possession should be imparted to his immediate relatives and friends."[337] DuPont reminisced about their time together at West Point, provided an overview of the battle and spoke with reverence regarding Ramseur's final hours. To DuPont, the interactions that he had with Ramseur on his deathbed signified reconciliation, just as his address at the monument dedication proved important to healing the conflict's wounds.

Following the Ramseur dedication in 1920, the numbers of veterans visiting the Valley decreased with each passing year as they answered their final roll call. While none can dispute the significance of the Battle of Cedar Creek from a political and military standpoint, perhaps the greatest role that Cedar Creek served was the healing of reconciliation, for without reconciliation the nation could never be truly restored and reunited. The reunions held on that battlefield until the early twentieth century, along with the three monument dedications, performed important work in healing the republic. Perhaps it was a member of the Sheridan's Veterans Association who in 1885 best captured the true meaning of the campaign of commemoration and reconciliation exhibited on the Valley's most significant field: "I am more than ready to put the past behind me, to look forward only. Our comrades of the gray are our fellow citizens. We should have, and I trust do have, one common purpose, one common hope—that the Union of our fathers may be preserved…let us clasp hands with our once brave foes, and all vie with each other in being true and loyal citizens of our common country."[338]

Notes

Introduction

1. *Exercises at the Dedication of the Monument Erected on the Battlefield at Cedar Creek, Virginia, by the Survivors of the 128th Regiment, N.Y.S.V.I., October 15, 1907* (N.p.: The Committee, n.d.), 7.

Chapter 1

2. For additional discussion of the Shenandoah Valley's agricultural productivity, see Michael G. Mahon, *The Shenandoah Valley 1861–1865: The Destruction of the Granary of the Confederacy* (Mechanicsburg, PA: Stackpole Books, 1999), 4–6.
3. The quintessential use of the Shenandoah Valley as a diversionary theater came during Stonewall Jackson's 1862 Valley Campaign. For further discussion of this campaign, see Peter Cozzens, *Shenandoah 1862: Stonewall Jackson's Valley Campaign* (Chapel Hill: University of North Carolina Press, 2008).
4. George N. Carpenter, *History of the Eighth Vermont Volunteers, 1861–1865* (Boston: Press of Deland and Barta, 1886), 164.
5. Ulysses S. Grant, *Personal Memoirs of U.S. Grant* (New York: Charles L. Webster & Co., 1886), 2: 316–17.
6. Mark A. Snell, *From First to Last: The Life of Major General William B. Franklin* (New York: Fordham University Press, 2002), 92, 151, 199.
7. Jeffry D. Wert, *The Sword of Lincoln: The Army of the Potomac* (New York: Simon & Schuster, 2005), 387; A. Wilson Greene, "Union Generalship in the 1864 Valley Campaign" in Gary W. Gallagher, ed., *Struggle for the Shenandoah: Essays on the 1864 Valley Campaign* (Kent, OH: Kent State University Press, 1991), 41–43.
8. Grant, *Personal Memoirs*, 2: 317.
9. General U. S. Grant to Sen. George F. Hoar, quoted in W.E. Woodward, *Meet General Grant* (U.S.: The Literary Guild of America, 1928), 261.
10. Charles Russell Lowell to wife, August 9, 1864, quoted in Edward Waldo Emerson, ed., *Life and Letters of Charles Russell Lowell: Captain, Sixth United States*

Cavalry, Colonel Second Massachusetts Cavalry, Brigadier-General, United States Volunteers (Columbia: University of South Carolina Press, 2005), 322.
11. Emory Upton to sister, August 9, 1864, quoted in Peter S. Michie, *The Life and Letters of Emory Upton: Colonel of the Fourth Regiment of Artillery, and Brevet-Major-General, U.S. Army* (New York: D. Appleton & Co., 1885), 122.
12. Harris Beecher, *Record of the 114th Regiment, NYSV: Where it Went, What it Saw, and What it Did* (Norwich, NY: J.F. Hubbard Jr., 1866), 396.
13. Orton S. Clark, *The One Hundred and Sixteenth Regiment of New York State Volunteers: Being a Complete History of Its Organization and of its Nearly Three Years of Active Service in the Great Rebellion* (Buffalo, NY: Printing House of Matthews and Warren, 1868), 205.
14. William Knowlton to wife, Harriet, August 9, 1864, William Knowlton Papers, Nicholas P. Picerno private collection, Bridgewater, VA.
15. Philip H. Sheridan, *Personal Memoirs of P.H. Sheridan* (New York: Charles L. Webster & Co., 1888), 1: 499–500.
16. Isaac O. Best, *History of the 121st New York State Infantry* (Chicago: Jas. H. Smith, 1921), 176.
17. For a more in-depth discussion of the Third Battle of Winchester, see Brandon H. Beck and Roger U. Delauter, *The Third Battle of Winchester* (Lynchburg, VA: H.E. Howard, 1997).
18. Mahon, *The Shenandoah Valley*, 135.
19. John O. Casler, *Four Years in the Stonewall Brigade* (Girard, KS: Appeal Publishing Co., 1906), 241.
20. John N. Opie, *A Rebel Cavalryman* (Chicago: W.B. Conkey, 1899), 254–55.
21. Clark, *The One Hundred and Sixteenth Regiment*, 238; For an excellent study of "The Burning," see John L. Heatwole, *The Burning: Sheridan in the Shenandoah Valley* (Charlottesville, VA: Rockbridge Publishing, 1998).
22. *New York Tribune*, September 21, 1864.
23. Rutherford B. Hayes to wife, October 12, 1864, quoted in Charles Richard Williams, ed., *Diary and Letters of Rutherford Birchard Hayes* (Columbus: Ohio State Archaeological and Historical Society, 1922), 2: 524.
24. Beecher, *Record of the 114th Regiment*, 442.
25. Clark, *The One Hundred and Sixteenth Regiment*, 238.
26. Ibid.
27. Ibid.
28. Jeffry D. Wert, *From Winchester to Cedar Creek: The Shenandoah Campaign of 1864* (Mechanicsburg, PA: Stackpole Books, 1997), 165–66.
29. George H. Nye to wife, October 13, 1864, papers of George H. Nye, 29th Maine Infantry, Nicholas P. Picerno private collection, Bridgewater, VA.

CHAPTER 2

30. General Jubal A. Early to Robert E. Lee, October 9, 1864, quoted in U.S. War Department, comp., *War of the Rebellion: A Compilation of the Official Records of the Union and Confederate Armies* (Washington, D.C.: Government Printing Office, 1880–1901), ser. 1, vol. 43, pt. 1, 559–60, hereafter cited as *O.R.*

31. Ibid., 579.
32. William S. Lincoln, *Life with the Thirty-Fourth Massachusetts Infantry in the War of the Rebellion* (Worcester, MA: Press of Noyes, Snow & Co., 1879), 371–72.
33. Ibid., 372.
34.. *O.R.*, ser. 1, vol. 43, pt. 1, 579.
35. Lincoln, *Life with the Thirty-Fourth Massachusetts*, 371.
36.. Ibid., 372. Casualty reports for fight of October 13, 1864.
37. Ibid., 374.
38. Ibid., 375.
39. Sheridan, *Personal Memoirs*, 2: 61.
40. Report of General Jubal A. Early, in *O.R.*, ser. 1, vol. 43, pt. 1, 561.
41. Benjamin F. Coates to wife, October 15, 1864, Coates Papers, Rutherford B. Hayes Presidential Center, Fremont, OH.
42. *O.R.*, ser. 1, vol. 43, pt. 1, 51.
43. Ibid., 51–52.
44. D. Augustus Dickert, *History of Kershaw's Brigade, With Complete Roll of Companies, Biographical Sketches, Incidents, Anecdotes, etc.* (Newberry, SC: Elbert H. Aull Co., 1899), 443.
45. Captain Samuel D. Buck, *With the Old Confeds: Actual Experiences of a Captain in the Line* (Baltimore, MD: H.E. Houck & Co., 1925), 122.
46. William Wartmann, quoted in George E. Pond, *The Shenandoah Valley in 1864* (New York: Charles Scribner's Sons, 1883), 200.
47. Jubal A. Early, *A Memoir of the Last Year of the War for Independence in the Confederate States of America* (Lynchburg, VA: Charles W. Button, 1867), 105.
48. Archie P. McDonald, ed., *Make Me a Map of the Valley: The Civil War Journal of Stonewall Jackson's Topographer* (Dallas: Southern Methodist University Press, 1973), 237; *O.R.*, ser. 1, vol. 43, pt. 1, 580.
49. Henry A. DuPont, *The Campaign of 1864 in the Valley of Virginia and the Expedition to Lynchburg* (New York: National Americana Society, 1925), 152.
50. Martin F. Schmitt, ed., *General George Crook: His Autobiography* (Norman: University of Oklahoma Press, 1946), 132.
51. George J. Howard to wife, October 20, 1864, George J. Howard Civil War Letters, Vermont Historical Society, Barre, VT.
52. McDonald, ed., *Make Me a Map of the Valley*, 238.
53. Richard B. Irwin, *History of the Nineteenth Army Corps* (New York: G.P. Putnam's Sons, 1892), 415–16.
54. George N. Carpenter, *History of the Eighth Regiment, Vermont Volunteers, 1861–1865* (Boston: Press of Deland and Barta, 1886), 207.
55. Benjamin W. Crowninshield, *The Battle of Cedar Creek: October 19, 1864, A Paper Read Before the Massachusetts Military Historical Society, December 8, 1879* (Cambridge, MA: Riverside Press, 1879), 10.
56. Ibid., 10–11.
57. Pond, *The Shenandoah Valley in 1864*, 312.
58. *O.R.*, ser. 1, vol. 43, pt. 1, 158.
59. Ibid., 333. Report of Colonel Edward Molineux.

60. Thomas A. Lewis, *The Guns of Cedar Creek* (New York: Harper & Row, 1988), 134.
61. Francis H. Buffum, *A Memorial of the Great Rebellion: Being a History of the Fourteenth Regiment New Hampshire Volunteers, Covering Its Three Years of Service, With Original Sketches of Army Life, 1861–1865* (Boston: Franklin Press, Rand, Avery, & Co., 1882), 278.
62. T. Harry Williams, *Hayes of the 23rd: The Civil War Volunteer Officer* (Lincoln: University of Nebraska Press, 1965), 287.
63. Dickert, *History of Kershaw's Brigade*, 445.
64. Terry L. Jones, ed., *The Civil War Memoirs of Captain William J. Seymour: Reminiscences of a Louisiana Tiger* (Baton Rouge: Louisiana State University Press, 1991), 148.
65. Buck, *With the Old Confeds*, 123.
66. Beecher, *Record of the 114th Regiment,* 443.
67. A.R. Rhoades to wife, October 18, 1864, from Cedar Creek Camp, A.R. Rhoades Papers, Rutherford B. Hayes Presidential Center, Fremont, OH.
68. Buffum, *A Memorial of the Great Rebellion*, 276.
69. Best, *History of the 121st New York State Infantry*, 189.

CHAPTER 3

70. Wert, *From Winchester to Cedar Creek*, 178; Schmitt, ed., *General George Crook,* 132; *O.R.* ser. 1, vol. 43, pt. 1, 382.
71. *O.R.,* ser. 1, vol. 43, pt. 1, 379.
72. Ibid., 522; Carol Bundy, *The Nature of Sacrifice: A Biography of Charles Russell Lowell, Jr., 1845–1864* (New York: Farar, Straus, and Giroux, 2005), 458; Theodore C. Mahr, *The Battle of Cedar Creek: Showdown in the Shenandoah, October 1–30, 1864* (Lynchburg, VA: H.E. Howard, 1992), 105.
73. Clifton Johnson, ed., *Battleground Adventures: The Stories of Dwellers on the Scenes of Conflict in Some of the Most Notable Battles of the Civil War* (Boston: Houghton Mifflin, 1915), 402.
74. *O.R.,* ser. 1, vol. 43, pt. 1, 407.
75. Ibid., 382.
76. Dickert, *History of Kershaw's Brigade,* 446.
77. *O.R.,* ser. 1, vol. 43, pt. 1, 591.
78. Dickert, *History of Kershaw's Brigade,* 448.
79. Ibid.
80. B.F. Cobb, unpublished postwar reminiscence about Battle of Cedar Creek, July 15, 1907, Thomas Cobb private collection, Elk Grove, CA.
81. Ibid.
82. *O.R.*, ser. 1, vol. 43, pt. 1, 418–20.
83. Cobb, unpublished postwar reminiscence about Battle of Cedar Creek, July 15, 1907, Thomas Cobb private collection, Elk Grove, CA.
84. *O.R.,* ser. 1, vol. 43, pt. 1, 419–21.

85. Alexander Neil to friends, October 21, 1864, quoted in Richard R. Duncan, ed., *Alexander Neil and the Shenandoah Valley Campaign: Letters of an Army Surgeon to His Family, 1864* (Shippensburg, PA: White Mane Publishing, 1996), 72.
86. This casualty estimate is based on the return of casualties from Thoburn's division during the Battle of Cedar Creek listed in *O.R.,* ser. 1, vol. 43, pt. 1, 135. The exact number of casualties reported for the division was 585.
87. Johnson, ed., *Battleground Adventures,* 403–04.
88. *O.R.*, ser. 1, vol. 43, pt. 1, 403; Williams, *Hayes of the 23rd*, 299.
89. Dickert, *History of Kershaw's Brigade,* 448.
90. Colonel Benjamin F. Coates to wife, October 19, 1864, Coates's Papers, Rutherford B. Hayes Presidential Center, Fremont, OH.
91. Homer B. Sprague, *History of the 13th Infantry Regiment of Connecticut Volunteers during the Great Rebelion* (Hartford, CT: Case, Lockwood, & Co., 1867), 238–39.
92. George J. Howard to wife, October 20, 1864, George J. Howard Civil War Letters, Vermont Historical Society, Barre, VT.
93. Reverend John R. Adams, *Memorial and Letters* (N.p.: Privately printed, 1890), 165.
94. *National Tribune,* July 19, 1894.
95. DuPont, *The Campaign of 1864 in the Valley of Virginia and the Expedition to Lynchburg*, 155.
96. *O.R.,* ser. 1, vol. 43, pt. 1, 374; Dennis E. Frye, Martin F. Graham and George F. Skoch, eds., *The James E. Taylor Sketchbook: With Sheridan Up the Shenandoah Valley in 1864, Leaves from a Special Artist's Sketchbook and Diary* (Dayton, OH: Morningside, 1989), 488.
97. C.J. Rawling, *History of the First Regiment West Virginia Infantry* (Philadelphia: J.B. Lippincott, 1887), 213.
98. *O.R.,* ser. 1, vol. 43, pt. 1, 404.
99. Gerald L. Earley, *I Belonged to the 116th: A Narrative of the 116th Ohio Volunteer Infantry during the Civil War* (Westminster, MD: Heritage Books, 2007), 175.
100. Thomas F. Wildes, *Record of the One Hundred and Sixteenth Ohio Infantry Volunteers in the War of the Rebellion* (Sandusky, OH: I.F. Mack & Bros., Printers, 1884), 205.
101. James H. Croushoure, ed., *A Volunteer's Adventures: A Union Captain's Record of the Civil War* (Baton Rouge: Louisiana State University Press, 1996), 208.
102. Beecher, *Record of the 114th Regiment,* 444.
103. D.H. Hanaburgh, *History of the One Hundred and Twenty-Eighth Regiment, New York Volunteers (U.S. Infantry) in the Late Civil War* (Poughkeepsie, NY: Press of Enterprise Publishing Co., 1894), 164.
104. Ibid.
105. Ibid., 164–65.
106. Joseph W.A. Whitehorne, *The Battle of Cedar Creek: Self-Guided Tour* (Middletown, VA: Cedar Creek Battlefield Foundation, 2006), 36. Whitehorne asserts that approximately twenty men from the 128th New York were captured near the intersection of the Valley Pike and Cedar Creek.
107. Johnson, ed., *Battleground Adventures*, 388.

108. Ibid., 388–89.
109. Whitehorne, *The Battle of Cedar Creek*, 36.
110. Beecher, *Record of the 114th Regiment*, 445.
111. Captain S.E. Howard, "The Morning Surprise at Cedar Creek," in *Civil War Papers Read Before the Commandery of the State of Massachusetts: Military Order Loyal Legion of the United States* (Boston: Published by the Commandery, 1900), 2:417–18.
112. Clark, *The One Hundred and Sixteenth Regiment*, 240.
113. See report of Colonel Edward L. Molineux in *O.R.*, ser. 1, vol. 43, pt. 1, 333.
114. Carpenter, *History of the Eighth Regiment Vermont Volunteers*, 209.
115. Ibid., 215.
116. Ibid., 218.
117. Howard, "The Morning Surprise at Cedar Creek," 419.
118. Ibid., 218.
119. Ibid. For casualty figures of Thomas's brigade at the Battle of Cedar Creek, see *O.R.*, ser. 1, vol. 43, pt. 1, 133.
120. Carpenter, *History of the Eighth Regiment Vermont Volunteers*, 210.
121. Hotchkiss to Carpenter, quoted in ibid., 212.
122. Phil S. Rogers, ed. *Everlasting Glory: Vermont Soldiers Who Were Awarded the Congressional Medal of Honor for Service During the Civil War 1861–1865* (Hardwick, VT: The Civil War Hemlocks, 2007), 55.
123. *O.R.*, ser. 1, vol. 43, pt. 1, 284.
124. Clark, *The One Hundred and Sixteenth Regiment*, 240.
125. Croushoure, ed., *A Volunteer's Adventures*, 215.
126. *O.R.*, ser. 1, vol. 43, pt. 1, 347–48.
127. Croushore, ed., *A Volunteer's Adventures*, 215.
128. Colonel Edward Molineux to sister, October 1864, Fred Molineux Private Collection, Pittstown, NJ.
129. John DeForrest, "Sheridan's Victory at Middletown" in *Harper's New Monthly Magazine* (New York: Harper & Brothers, 1865), 30: 355.
130. *O.R.*, ser. 1, vol. 43, pt. 1, 342.
131. William F. Tiemann, *The 159th Regiment, New York State Volunteers* (Brooklyn, NY: William F. Tiemann, 1891), 107.
132. Reverend James K. Ewer, *The Third Massachusetts Cavalry in the War for the Union* (Maplewood, MA: Historical Comm. of the Regimental Association, 1903), 221.
133. Croushoure, ed., *A Volunteer's Adventures*, 216.
134. Joseph Warren Keifer, *Slavery and Four Years of War: A Political History of Slavery in the United States Together with a Narrative of the Campaigns and Battles of the Civil War in Which the Author Took Part, 1861–1865* (New York: G.P. Putnam's Sons, 1900), 2: 132.
135. *National Tribune*, November 24, 1887.
136. Best, *History of the 121st New York State Infantry*, 189.
137. Buffum, *A Memorial of the Great Rebellion*, 281.
138. *National Tribune*, November 24, 1887.

139. Wildes, *Record of the One Hundred Sixteenth Ohio*, 207.
140. Ibid.
141. Ibid.
142. Benjamin W. Crowninshield, *The Battle of Cedar Creek: October 19, 1864, A Paper Read Before the Military Historical Society of Massachusetts, December 8, 1879* (Cambridge, MA: Riverside Press, 1879), 21-22.
143. Ibid.
144. DeForrest, "Sheridan's Victory at Middletown," 357.
145. Stevens, quoted in Penrose G. Mark, *Red: White: and Blue Badge: Pennsylvania Veteran Volunteers, A History of the 93rd Regiment, Known as the "Lebanon Infantry" and "One of the 300 Fighting Regiments" from September 12th 1861 to June 27th, 1865* (Harrisburg, PA: The Aughinbaugh Press, 1911), 301.
146. Keifer, *Slavery and Four Years of War*, 2:133.
147. *O.R.,* ser. 1, vol. 43, pt. 1, 251.
148. Keifer, *Slavery and Four Years of War*, 2:134.
149. Ibid., 136; Wert, *From Winchester to Cedar Creek*, 200.
150. Keifer, *Slavery and Four Years of War*, 2:135–36.
151. Aldace F. Walker, *The Vermont Brigade in the Shenandoah Valley, 1864* (Burlington, VT: The Free Press Association, 1869), 141.
152. Ibid., 142.
153. *O.R.,* ser. 1, vol. 43, pt. 1, 599.
154. Walker, *The Vermont Brigade in the Shenandoah Valley*, 144; Whitehorne, *Battle of Cedar Creek*, 43.
155. Johnson, ed., *Battleground Adventures,* 408.
156. Hillman A. Hall, W.B. Besley and Gilbert G. Wood, *History of the Sixth New York Cavalry (Second Ira Harris Guard): Second Brigade-First Division-Cavalry Corps, Army of the Potomac, 1861–1865, Compiled from Letters, Diaries, Recollections and Official Records* (Worcester, MA: The Blanchard Press, 1908), 235.
157. *O.R.,* ser. 1, vol. 43, pt. 1, 478.
158. Wert, *From Winchester to Cedar Creek*, 215. In his book, Wert states that troops from Wharton's command and Brigadier General William Wofford's command ran into the Union cavalry. Wofford was not at Cedar Creek, but his brigade commanded by Colonel Henry P. Sanders, a part of Kershaw's division, was at the battle.
159. *O.R.,* ser. 1, vol. 43, pt. 1, 562.
160. Dickert, *History of Kershaw's Brigade*, 449.
161. Daniel Allen Wilson to unidentified addressee, October 21, 1864, Beverly Randolph Wellford Papers, 1773–1907, Virginia Historical Society, Richmond, VA.
162. John H. Worsham, *One of Jackson's Foot Cavalry: His Experience and What He Saw During the War 1861–1865* (New York: The Neale Publishing Co., 1912), 276–77.
163. General Jubal A. Early, *Autobiographical Sketch and Narrative of the War Between the States* (Philadelphia: J.B. Lippincott, 1912), 447–48.
164. William H. Runge, ed., *Four Years in the Confederate Artillery: The Diary of Private Henry Robinson Berkeley* (Richmond: Virginia Historical Society, 1991), 106.

165. Henry Kyd Douglas, *I Rode with Stonewall* (Marietta, GA: Mockingbird Books, 1995), 303.
166. General John B. Gordon, *Reminiscences of the Civil War* (New York: Charles Scribner's Sons, 1904), 341–42.
167. Randolph H. McKim, *A Soldier's Recollections: Leaves from the Diary of a Young Confederate* (New York: Longman's, Green, and Co., 1910), 237.
168. E. Ruffin Harris, "Battle Near Cedar Creek, Va," *Confederate Veteran* 9, no. 9 (1901): 390.
169. Beecher, *Record of the 114th Regiment*, 447–48.
170. George W. Powers, *The Story of the Thirty-Eighth Regiment of Massachusetts Volunteers* (Cambridge, MA: Cambridge Press, Dakin and Metcalf, 1866), 172.
171. William B. Jordan, ed., *The Civil War Journals of John Mead Gould: 1861–1866* (Baltimore, MD: Butternut & Blue, 1997), 422.
172. Beecher, *Record of the 114th Regiment*, 448.

CHAPTER 4

173. Robert Hunt Rhodes, ed., *All for the Union: The Civil War Diary and Letters of Elisha Hunt Rhodes* (New York: Vintage Books, 1985), 184.
174. Sheridan, *Personal Memoirs*, 2: 68–69.
175. General George A. Forsyth, "Sheridan's Ride" *Harper's New Monthly Magazine* (July 1897), 168.
176. Sheridan, *Personal Memoirs*, 2: 69–71.
177. Ibid.
178. Forsyth, "Sheridan's Ride," 168.
179. Ibid., 171–72.
180. Philip H. Sheridan address to graduating class, West Point, 1878, Philip H. Sheridan Papers, Roll 100, Library of Congress, Washington, D.C.
181. Sheridan, *Personal Memoirs,* 2: 82.
182. John M. Gould, *History of the First-Tenth-Twenty-Ninth Maine Regiment* (Portland, ME: Stephen Berry, 1871), 537.
183. Lieutenant Edward Duffy, *History of the 159th Regiment, N.Y.S.V. Compiled from the Diary of Lt. Edward Duffy* (New York: 1890), 36.
184. Sheridan, *Personal Memoirs*, 2: 85–86.
185. Thomas H. M'Cann, *The Campaigns of the Civil War in the United States of America, 1861–1865* (Hudson County, NJ: Hudson Observer, 1915), 196.
186. Beecher, *Record of the 114th Regiment*, 449.
187. Powers, *38th Massachusetts*, 172.
188. Buck, *With the Old Confeds*, 126.
189. Runge, ed., *Four Years in the Confederate Artillery*, 106.
190. Beecher, *Record of the 114th Regiment*, 449.
191. Sheridan, *Personal Memoirs*, 2: 86.
192. Early, *A Memoir of the Last Year of the War,* 115.
193. DeForrest, "Sheridan's Victory at Middletown," 358.

194. Hanaburgh, *History of the One Hundred and Twenty-Eighth Regiment*, 168.
195. Worsham, *One of Jackson's Foot Cavalry*, 277.
196. DeForrest, "Sheridan's Victory at Middletown," 358.
197. Early, *A Memoir of the Last Year of the War for Independence*, 115.
198. Captain J.S. McNeilly, "Battle of Cedar Creek," *Southern Historical Society Papers* 32 (1904): 232. For an additional discussion of the "fatal halt" at Cedar Creek see Keith S. Bohannon, "'The Fatal Halt' versus 'Bad Conduct': John B. Gordon, Jubal Early, and the Battle of Cedar Creek" in Gary W. Gallagher, ed., *The Shenandoah Valley Campaign of 1864* (Chapel Hill: University of North Carolina Press, 2006), 56–84.
199. Sheridan, *Personal Memoirs*, 2: 88.
200. Gordon, *Reminiscences*, 346; Mahr, *The Battle of Cedar Creek*, 272.
201. General A. Bayard Nettleton, "How the Day was Saved at the Battle of Cedar Creek," *Glimpses of the Nation's Struggle: A Series of Papers Read Before the Minnesota Commandery of the Military Order of the Loyal Legion of the United States* (St. Paul, MN: St. Paul Book and Stationary Co., 1887), 271.
202. Gould, *First-Tenth-Twenty-Ninth Maine*, 539.
203. Carpenter, *History of the Eighth Vermont*, 220.
204. Mahr, *The Battle of Cedar Creek*, 276.
205. Walker, *The Vermont Brigade*, 150.
206. Colonel Benjamin W. Crowninshield, *The Battle of Cedar Creek, October 19, 1864* (Cambridge: Riverside Press, 1879), 28.
207. Keifer, *Slavery and Four Years of War*, 2: 146.
208. Military Historical Society of Massachusetts, *The Shenandoah Campaigns of 1862 and 1864*, 133.
209. Early, *Narrative of the War Between the States*, 448.
210. Dwight had been under arrest by Sheridan's order for refusing to revise his official report about the Third Battle of Winchester, which was extremely critical of General Cuvier Grover.
211. *O.R.*, ser. 1, vol. 43, pt. 1, 310.
212. Gould, *History of the First-Tenth-Twenty-Ninth Maine*, 540.
213. Carpenter, *History of the Eighth Vermont*, 223.
214. Buffum, *A Memorial of the Great Rebellion*, 289–90.
215. Early, *Narrative of the War Between the States*, 448.
216. Beecher, *114th New York*, 452.
217. Ibid.
218. Clark, *The One Hundred and Sixteenth Regiment*, 246–47.
219. *O.R.*, ser. 1, vol. 43, pt. 1, 43, 524.
220. Gordon, *Reminiscences of the Civil War*, 348.
221. Buffum, *A Memorial of the Great Rebellion*, 289.
222. Daniel Allen Wilson to unidentified recipient, October 21, 1864, Beverly Randolph Wellford Papers, 1773–1907, Section 112, Virginia Historical Society, Richmond, VA.
223. Early, *Narrative of the War Between the States*, 448.
224. Walker, *Vermont Brigade*, 151.

225. William R. Cox, "Major-General Stephen D. Ramseur: His Life and Character," *Southern Historical Society Papers* 18 (1890): 254.
226. Early, *Narrative of the War Between the States*, 450.
227. *O.R.*, ser. 1, vol. 43, pt. 1, 450.
228. *Memoirs of the War of '61: Colonel Charles Russell Lowell, Friends and Cousins* (Boston: Press of Geo. H. Ellis, Co., 1920), 11.
229. *O.R.*, ser. 1, vol. 43, pt. 1, 451.
230. *Harper's Weekly*, November 5, 1864.
231. Moses M. Granger, "The Battle of Cedar Creek," in Robert Hunter, ed., *Sketches of War History, 1861–1865* (Cincinnati: Robert Clarke & Co., 1890), 134.
232. Walker, *The Vermont Brigade*, 152.
233. Ibid., 152.
234. Buffum, *A Memorial of the Great Rebellion*, 290.
235. Walker, *The Vermont Brigade*, 152.
236. Johnson, ed., *Battleground Adventures*, 390.
237. Whitehorne, *Battle of Cedar Creek*, 31; A Union account noted that a plank or two on the bridge were broken and that prevented the rolling stock from passing over the bridge safely. See "Cedar Creek" in *Papers of the Military Historical Society of Massachusetts: The Shenandoah Campaigns of 1862 and 1864 and the Appomattox Campaign 1865* (Boston: Military Historical Society of Massachusetts, 1907), 175.
238. Dickert, *History of Kershaw's Brigade*, 452.
239. Ibid., 453.
240. W.F. Beyer and O.F. Keydel, eds., *Deeds of Valor* (Detroit: The Perrien-Keydel Co., 1906), 1: 447.
241. A Surgeon in the Confederate Army, "The Battle of Cedar Creek," *Southern Historical Society Papers* 16 (1888), 446.
242. Beyer and Keydel, eds., *Deeds of Valor*, 1: 448; Phil S. Rogers, ed., *Everlasting Glory: Vermont Soldiers who were Awarded the Congressional Medal of Honor for Service During the Civil War 1861–1865* (Hardwick: The Vermont Civil War Hemlocks, 2007), 60.
243. Henry A. Dupont, *Address by Colonel DuPont Upon the Unveiling of Major General Ramseur's Monument* (Winterthur, DE: Henry A. Dupont, 1920), 12–13.
244. Cox, "Major-General Stephen D. Ramseur," 257–58.
245. John K. Bucklyn, *Battle of Cedar Creek* (Providence, RI: Sidney S. Rider, 1883), 19.
246. George Stevens, *Three Years in the Sixth Corps: A Concise Narrative of Events in the Army of the Potomac, From 1861 to the Close of the Rebellion, April, 1865* (Albany, NY: S.R. Gray, Publishers, 1866), 426.
247. Description of Battle of Cedar Creek, Alfred Rigby, 28th Iowa Infantry, Cedar Creek Battlefield Foundation Archives, Middletown, VA.
248. Adams, *Memorial and Letters*, 166.
249. Charles H. Anson, "Battle of Cedar Creek, October 19th, 1864," in *War Papers Read Before the Commandery of the State of Wisconsin, Military Order of the Loyal Legion of the United States* (Milwaukee, WI: Burick and Allen, 1914), 365–66.

250. Jordan, ed., *The Civil War Journals of John Mead Gould*, 423.
251. Colonel Edward Molineux to sister Nan, October 19, 1864, Fred Molineux private collection, Pittstown, NJ.
252. Peter P. Boarts to parents, October 21, 1864, Civil War Misc. Collection, Peter P. Boarts Letter Archives, 22nd Iowa, United States Army Military History Institute, Carlisle, PA.
253. Casualty figures are based off information from George E. Pond, *The Shenandoah Valley in 1864*, 239–40.
254. Colonel Edward Molineux to sister Nan, October 20, 1864, Fred Molineux private collection, Pittstown, NJ.
255. Stevens, *Three Years in the Sixth Corps*, 427.
256. Keifer, *Slavery and Four Years of War*, 2: 153.
257. Shull Reminiscences, Box 14, Belle Grove Collection, Stewart Bell Jr., Archives, Handley Regional Library, Winchester, VA.
258. Johnson, ed., *Battleground Adventures*, 390.
259. Keifer, *Slavery and Four Years of War*, 2: 153.
260. Johnson, ed., *Battleground Adventures*, 416. The identity of this man is not known. He is simply identified by Johnson, who conducted this postwar interview, as "The Black Fiddler."
261. Ibid., 390.
262. Colonel Edward Molineux to sister Nan, October 20, 1864, Fred Molineux private collection, Pittstown, NJ.
263. Early, *Narrative of the War Between the States*, 451.
264. *O.R.*, ser. 1, vol. 43, pt. 1, 563.
265. Daniel Allen Wilson to unidentified recipient, October 21, 1864, Beverly Randolph Wellford Papers, 1773–1907, Virginia Historical Society, Richmond, VA.
266. Buck, *With the Old Confeds*, 127.
267. Schmitt, ed., *General George Crook*, 134.

CHAPTER 5

268. George E. Baker, ed., *The Works of William H. Seward* (Boston: Houghton Mifflin, 1890), 5:161.
269. John G. Nicolay and John Hay, eds., *Complete Works of Abraham Lincoln* (New York: Francis D. Tandy, 1905), 10: 251.
270. Margaret Leech, *Reveille in Washington: 1860–1865* (New York: Harper and Brothers, 1941), 351.
271. Roy P. Basler, ed., *The Collected Works of Abraham Lincoln* (New Brunswick, NJ: Rutgers University Press, 1953), 8: 58–59; For further reading on the political situation Lincoln confronted in 1864, see Charles Bracelen Flood, *1864: Lincoln at the Gates of History* (New York: Simon & Schuster, 2009).
272. Flood, *1864: Lincoln at the Gates of History*, 350–51; *Harper's Weekly*, November 12, 1864.
273. James M. McPherson, *Tried by War: Abraham Lincoln as Commander-in-Chief* (New York: The Penguin Press, 2008), 250–51.

274. *O.R.*, ser. 1, vol. 43, pt. 1, 62.
275. *New York Evening Post*, October 25, 1864.
276. *New York Tribune*, October 25, 1864.
277. *Baltimore American and Commercial Advertiser*, October 27, 1864.
278. *New York Herald*, October 24, 1864.
279. *Harper's Weekly*, November 5, 1864.
280. Frank A. Burr and Richard J. Hinton, *The Life of Gen. Philip H. Sheridan: Its Romance and Reality* (Providence, RI: J.A. & R.A. Reid Publishers, 1888), 230–32.
281. "Sheridan's Ride," *Chicago Inter Ocean*, newspaper clipping in Thomas Buchanan Read Papers, Beinecke Rare Books and Manuscripts Library, Yale University, New Haven, CT. Items from this collection cited hereafter as TBR.
282. "The Murdoch Testimonial Last Night: Tuesday, November 1, 1864," TBR.
283. Burr and Hinton, *The Life of Gen. Philip H. Sheridan*, 233.
284. John Fleischman, "The Object at Hand," *Smithsonian*, November 1996, 30.
285. Joseph E. Suppiger, "Rienzi," *Lincoln Herald* no. 3 (81), 196.
286. Fleischmann, "The Object at Hand," 30.
287. Gary W. Gallagher, ed., *The Shenandoah Valley Campaign of 1864* (Chapel Hill: University of North Carolina Press, 2006), 23.
288. "Academy of the Fine Arts. The Great National Painting, Sheridan's Ride, by T. Buchanan Read, Now on Exhibition," 7, pamphlet in collection of Macculoch Hall Historical Museum, Morristown, NJ.
289. James G. Barber, ed., *Faces of Discord: The Civil War Era at the National Portrait Gallery* (New York: Smithsonian, 2006), 203.
290. "A Visit to Sheridan's Ride," *Punchinello* no. 3, 1 (1870), 46.
291. Captain Laurence Kip on Read's "Sheridan's Ride," in "Academy of the Fine Arts," 13.
292. Sheridan's reaction to Thulstrup's painting is based off of "A Misrepresentation," newspaper clipping, Scott Patchan, private collection, Haymarket, VA.
293. *Illustrated and Descriptive Catalogue of "Sheridan's Ride" Andrus Great War Painting, 1890*, 17, booklet in collection of Vermont Veterans Militia Museum and Library, Colchester, VT.
294. Advertisement for First National Bank of Yarmouth; Advertisement for the Boston Mutual, Jonathan A. Noyalas, private collection, Martinsburg, WV.
295. T.C. DeLeon, *Crag-Nest: A Romance of the Days of Sheridan's Ride* (New York: G.W. Dillingham Co. Publishers, 1910), vii.
296. Joseph D. Shewalter, "Observations on Sheridan's Ride," *Confederate Veteran* 23, no. 3 (1923): 88.
297. Victor L. Thacker, ed., *French Harding: Civil War Memoirs* (Parsons, WV: McClain Printing Co., 2000), 178.
298. Gould, *First-Tenth-Twenty-ninth Maine*, 550.
299. Thomas Wentworth Higginson, *Young Folks' Story of the United States* (Boston: Lee and Shephard Publishers, 1887), 312–13.
300. Russell Hastings Memoirs, 23, Russell Hastings Papers, Rutherford B. Hayes Presidential Library, Fremont, OH.

301. *Proceedings of the Senate and Assembly of the State of New York, on the Life and Services of Gen. Philip H. Sheridan, Held at the Capitol, April 9, 1889* (Albany, NY: James B. Lyon, State Printer, 1890), 38, 40.
302. *A Memorial of Philip Henry Sheridan from the City of Boston* (Boston: Printed by Order of the City Council, 1889), 24.
303. Burr and Hinton, *The Life of Gen. P.H. Sheridan*, 411.
304. Colonel Herbert E. Hill, *Campaign in the Shenandoah Valley, 1864: A Paper Read Before the Eighth Vermont Volunteers and First Vermont Cavalry, at Their Annual Reunion, in Montpelier, Vermont, November 2, 1886* (Boston: Published by the Executive Committee, 1886), 11.

CHAPTER 6

305. Hill, *Campaign in the Shenandoah Valley, 1864*, 3, 7.
306. John O. Casler, *Four Years in the Stonewall Brigade* (Girard, KS: Appeal Publishing Co., 1906), 241.
307. Kenneth E. Koons, "The Colored Laborers Work as Well as When Slaves: African Americans in the Breadbasket of the Confederacy, 1850–1880," in Clarence R. Geier and Stephen R. Potter, eds., *Archaeological Perspectives on the American Civil War* (Gainesville: University Press of Florida, 2000), 241–42.
308. Francis Henry Buffum, *Sheridan's Veterans No. II: A Souvenir of their Third Campaign in the Shenandoah Valley, 1864–1883–1885, September 15–25, 1885* (Boston: W.F. Brown & Co., 1886), 97.
309. W.C. King and W.P. Derby, comps., *Camp-Fire Sketches and Battle-Field Echoes* (Springfield, MA: King, Richardson, and Co., 1886), 513. For additional discussion of a changing view of the South from a battlefield into a spot for vacation, see Nina Silber, *The Romance of Reunion: Northerners and the South, 1865–1900* (Chapel Hill: University of North Carolina Press, 1993), 66–70. For additional discussions on the emergence of postwar reconciliation see David W. Blight, *Race and Reunion: The Civil War in American Memory* (Cambridge: Belknap Press, 2001), 198–206; Thomas J. Brown, *The Public Art of Civil War Commemoration: A Brief History with Documents* (Boston: Bedford St. Martins, 2004), 3–7.
310. Francis Henry Buffum, *Sheridan's Veterans: A Souvenir of their Two Campaigns in the Shenandoah Valley, the One, of War, in 1864, the Other, of Peace, in 1883, Being the Record of the Excursion to the Battle-Fields of the Valley of Virginia, September 15–25, 1883* (Boston: W.F. Brown and Co., Printers, 1883), vii.
311. *Spirit of Jefferson*, September 25, 1883.
312. Speech of Colonel Carroll D. Wright, September 18, 1883, quoted in Buffum, *Sheridan's Veterans…1883*, 23.
313. Buffum, *Sheridan's Veterans…1883*, 87.
314. Ibid., 89.
315. *Winchester News*, September 1883.
316. Buffum, *Sheridan's Veterans No. II*, 86.
317. Ibid.
318. Ibid., 88.

319. Ibid., 89.
320. Ibid.
321. Ibid., 92.
322. Ibid., 95.
323. Ibid., 99.
324. Fitzhugh Lee to Veterans at Winchester, September 18, 1885, quoted in *Winchester Times*, September 23, 1885.
325. Buffum, *Sheridan's Veterans No. II*, 34.
326. Ibid., 100.
327. Ibid., 101.
328. *The Evening Enterprise*, October 12, 1907.
329. Ibid.
330. *Exercises at the Dedication of a Monument Erected on the Battlefield of Cedar Creek, Virginia by the Survivors of the 128th Regiment, N.Y.S. V.I, October 15, 1907* (N.p.: Published by the Committee, n.d.), 4.
331. Ibid., 6.
332. Ibid., 9.
333. Ibid., 13–14.
334. Ibid., 14–15.
335. *News and Observer, Raleigh, N.C.,* September 17, 1920, newspaper clipping in the Monuments and Memorials Collection, Museum of the Confederacy, Richmond, VA; "Program for the Dedication of the Ramseur Memorial," Monuments and Memorials Collection, Museum of the Confederacy, Richmond, VA.
336. *Winchester Evening Star,* September 16, 1920.
337. Henry A. DuPont, *Address by Colonel DuPont Upon the Unveiling of Major General Ramseur's Monument* (Winterthur, DE: H.A. DuPont, 1920), 1–2.
338. Buffum, *Sheridan's Veterans No. II*, 52–53.

Bibliography

Manuscript Collections

Beinecke Rare Book and Manuscripts Library, Yale University, New Haven, CT
Thomas Buchanan Read Papers

Fred Molineux, Pittstown, NJ
Colonel Edward Molineux Papers

Jonathan A. Noyalas, Martinsburg, WV
Sheridan's Ride Materials
Sheridan's Veterans Materials

Library of Congress, Washington, D.C.
Abraham Lincoln Papers
Philip H. Sheridan Papers

Macculloch Hall Historical Museum, Morristown, NJ
"Sheridan's Ride"—Poem and Announcement of Painting, T.B. Read

Museum of the Confederacy, Richmond, VA
Monuments and Memorials Collection

Nicholas P. Picerno, Bridgewater, VA
George Nye Papers
Sheridan's Veterans Materials
William Knowlton Papers

Rutherford B. Hayes's Presidential Center, Fremont, OH
Benjamin F. Coates Papers
Rhoades Papers
Russell Hastings Papers

Scott Patchan, Haymarket, VA
General Philip H. Sheridan materials

Stewart Bell Jr. Archives, Handley Regional Library, Winchester, VA
Belle Grove Collection

United States Army Military History Institute, Carlisle, PA
Civil War Times Illustrated Collection
Crook-Kennon Papers
Harrisburg Civil War Roundtable Collection

Vermont Historical Society, Barre, VT
George J. Howard Civil War Letters

Vermont Veterans Militia Museum and Library, Colchester, VT
Charles H. Andrus Papers
Sheridan's Ride Materials

Virginia Historical Society, Richmond, VA
Beverly Randolph Wellford Papers, 1773–1907
Thomas Henry Carter Papers, 1861–1904

Government Documents

U.S. War Department, comp. *War of the Rebellion: A Compilation of the Official Records of the Union and Confederate Armies.* 128 vols. Washington, D.C.: U.S. Government Printing Office, 1880–1901.

Published Primary Sources

Adams, Reverend John R. *Memorial and Letters*. N.p.: privately printed, 1890.

Anson, Charles H. "Battle of Cedar Creek, October 19th, 1864," in *War Papers Read Before the Commandery of the State of Wisconsin, Military Order of the Loyal Legion of the United States*. Milwaukee, WI: Burick and Allen, 1914.

Basler, Roy P., ed. *The Collected Works of Abraham Lincoln*. 8 vols. New Brunswick, NJ: Rutgers University Press, 1953.

Beach, William H. *The First New York (Lincoln) Cavalry, From April 19, 1861 to July 7, 1865*. Reprint. Annandale, VA: Bacon Race, 1988.

Beecher, Harris H. *Record of the 114th Regiment, N.Y.S.V.* Norwich, NY: J.F. Hubbard, Jr., 1866.

Best, Isaac O. *History of the 121st New York State Infantry*. Chicago: Jas. H. Smith, 1921.

Beyer, W.F., and O.F. Keydel, eds. *Deeds of Valor*. vol. 1. Detroit: The Perrien-Keydel Co., 1906.

Buck, Captain Samuel D. *With the Old Confeds: Actual Experiences of a Captain in the Line*. Baltimore, MD: H.E. Houck & Co., 1925.

Buffum, F.H. *Sheridan's Veterans: A Souvenir of Their Two Campaigns in the Shenandoah Valley, The One, of War, in 1864, The Other, of Peace, in 1883, Being the Record of the Excursion to the Battle-Fields of the Valley of Virginia, September 15–24, 1883*. Boston: W.F. Brown and Co., Printers, 1883.

———. *Sheridan's Veterans No. II: A Souvenir of Their Third Campaign in the Shenandoah Valley, 1864–1883–1885, September 15–24, 1885.* Boston: W.F. Brown and Co., Printers, 1886.

Carpenter, George N. *History of the Eighth Vermont Volunteers, 1861–1865*. Boston: Press of Deland and Barta, 1886.

Casler, John O. *Four Years in the Stonewall Brigade*. Girard, KS: Appeal Publishing, 1906.

Citizens of Albany and State of New York. *Unveiling of the Equestrian Statue of General Philip H. Sheridan, Capital Park, Albany, New York, October 1916.* N.p.: n.d.

Clark, Orton S. *One Hundred and Sixteenth New York Volunteers*. Buffalo, NY: Printing House of Matthews and Warren, 1868.

Croushoure, James H., ed. *A Volunteer's Adventures: A Union Captain's Record of The Civil War*. Baton Rouge: Louisiana State University Press, 1996.

Crowninshield, Benjamin W. *The Battle of Cedar Creek: October 19, 1864, A Paper Read Before the Massachusetts Military Historical Society, December 8, 1879*. Cambridge, MA: Riverside Press, 1879.

DeForrest, John. "Sheridan's Victory at Middletown." *Harper's New Monthly Magazine*. New York: Harper & Brothers, 1865.

Dickert, D. Augustus. *History of Kershaw's Brigade, with Complete Roll of Companies, Biographical Sketches, Incidents, Anecdotes, etc.* Newberry, SC: Elbert H. Aull Co., 1899.

Donald, David Herbert, ed. *Inside Lincoln's Cabinet: The Civil War Diaries of Salmon P. Chase*. New York: Longmans Green, 1954.

Douglas, Henry Kyd. *I Rode with Stonewall*. Marietta, GA: Mockingbird Books, 1995.

Duffy, Lieutenant Edward. *History of the 159th Regiment, N.Y.S.V. Compiled from the Diary of Lt. Edward Duffy*. New York: 1890.

Duncan, Richard R., ed. *Alexander Neil and the Last Shenandoah Valley Campaign: Letters of an Army Surgeon to his Family, 1864*. Shippensburg, PA: WhiteMane Publishing, 1996.

DuPont, Henry A. *Address by Colonel DuPont Upon the Unveiling of Major General Ramseur's Monument*. Winterthur, DE: Henry A. DuPont, 1920.

———. *The Campaign of 1864 in the Valley of Virginia and the Expedition to Lynchburg*. New York: National Americana Society, 1925.

Early, Jubal A. *Autobiographical Sketch and Narrative of the War Between the States.* Philadelphia: J.B. Lippincott, 1912.

———. *A Memoir of the Last Year of the War for Independence in the Confederate States of America*. Lynchburg, VA: Charles W. Button, 1867.

Eddy, Richard. *History of the Sixtieth Regiment New York State Volunteers*. Philadelphia: Self-published, 1864.

Emerson, Edward Waldo, ed. *Life and Letters of Charles Russell Lowell: Captain, Sixth United States Cavalry, Colonel, Second Massachusetts Cavalry, Brigadier-General, United States Volunteers*. Columbia: University of South Carolina Press, 2005.

Ewer, James K. *The Third Massachusetts Cavalry in the War for the Union*. Maplewood, MA: Historical Committee of the Regimental Association, 1903.

Exercises at the Dedication of the Monument Erected on the Battlefield at Cedar Creek, Virginia, by the Survivors of the 128th Regiment, N.Y.S. V.I., October 15, 1907. N.p.: The Committee, n.d.

Flinn, Frank M. *Campaigning with Banks in Louisiana, '63 and '64, and with Sheridan in the Shenandoah Valley in '64 and '65*. Boston: W.B. Clarke, 1889.

Forsyth, George A. *Thrilling Days in Army Life*. New York: Harper and Brothers, 1900.

Frye, Dennis E., Martin F. Graham and George F. Skoch, eds. *The James E. Taylor Sketchbook: With Sheridan Up the Shenandoah Valley in 1864, Leave from a Special Artist's Sketch Book and Diary*. Dayton, OH: Morningside, 1989.

Grant, U.S. *Personal Memoirs of U.S. Grant*. 2 vols. New York: Charles L. Webster & Co., 1886.

Hanaburgh, David Henry. *History of the One Hundred and Twenty-Eighth Regiment New York Volunteers (U.S. Infantry) in the Late Civil War*. Poughkeepsie, NY: Press of Enterprise Publishing Co., 1894.

Hill, Colonel Herbert E. *Campaigning in the Shenandoah Valley, 1864: A Paper Read Before the Eighth Vermont Volunteers and First Vermont Cavalry, at their Annual Re-union, in Montpelier, Vermont, November 2, 1886*. Boston: Published by the Executive Committee, 1886.

Howard, Captain S.E. "The Morning Surprise at Cedar Creek," in *Civil War Papers Read Before the Commandery of the State of Massachusetts: Military Order Loyal Legion of the United States*. Boston: Published by the Commandery, 1900.

Hunter, Robert, ed. *Sketches of War History, 1861–1865*. Cincinnati, OH: Robert Clarke & Co., 1890.

Irwin, Richard B. *History of the Nineteenth Army Corps*. New York: G.P. Putnam's Sons, 1892.

Johnson, Clifton, comp. *Battleground Adventures: The Stories of Dwellers on the Scenes of Conflict of Some of the Most Notable Battles of the Civil War*. Boston: Houghton Mifflin, 1915.

Johnson, Mary E., ed. *From a "whirlpool of death...to victory": Civil War Remembrances of Jesse Tyler Sturm 14th West Virginia Infantry*. Charleston: West Virginia History, 2002.

Jordan, William B., ed. *The Civil War Journals of John Mead Gould: 1861–1866*. Baltimore, MD: Butternut & Blue, 1997.

Kallgren, Beverly Hayes, and James L. Crouthamel, eds. *"Dear Friend Anna": The Civil War Letters of a Common Soldier from Maine*. Orono: The University of Maine Press, 1992.

Keifer, Joseph Warren. *Slavery and Four Years of War: A Political History of Slavery in the United States together with a Narrative of the Campaigns and Battles of the Civil War in which the Author Took Part.* 2 vols. New York: Putnam, 1900.

Kennon, Lieutenant L.W.V. "The Valley Campaign of 1864: A Military Study." *Shenandoah Campaigns of 1862 and 1864 and the Appomattox Campaign, 1865.* Vol. 6. Boston: Military Historical Society of Massachusetts, 1907.

King, W.C., comp. *Camp-Fire Sketches and Battlefield Echoes of the Rebellion.* Springfield, MA: W.C. King and Co., 1887.

Mark, Penrose G. *Red: White: and Blue Badge: Pennsylvania Veteran Volunteers: A History of the 93rd Regiment, Known as the "Lebanon Infantry" and "One of the 300 Fighting Regiments" from September 12th 1861 to June 27th, 1865.* Harrisburg, PA: Aughinbaugh Press, 1911.

Mathless, Paul, ed. *Voices of the Civil War: Shenandoah 1864.* Alexandria, VA: Time Life Books, 1998.

M'Cann, Thomas H. *The Campaigns of the Civil War in the United States of America, 1861–1865.* Hudson County, NJ: Hudson Observer, 1915.

McDonald, Archie P., ed. *Make Me a Map of the Valley: The Civil War Journal of Stonewall Jackson's Topographer, Jedediah Hotchkiss.* Dallas: Southern Methodist University Press, 1989.

A Memorial of Philip Henry Sheridan from the City of Boston. Boston: Printed by Order of the City Council, 1889.

Michie, Peter S. *The Life and Letters of Emory Upton: Colonel of the Fourth Regiment of Artillery, and Brevet-Major General, U.S. Army.* New York: D. Appleton & Co., 1885.

Military Historical Society of Massachusetts. *The Shenandoah Campaigns of 1862 and 1864 and the Appomattox Campaign, 1865.* Boston: The Military Historical Society of Massachusetts, 1907.

Nettleton, Gen. A. Bayard. "How the Day was Saved at the Battle of Cedar Creek." In *Glimpses of the Nation's Struggle: A Series of Papers Read Before the Minnesota Commandery of the Military Order of the Loyal Legion of the United States.* St. Paul, MN: St. Paul Book and Stationary Co., 1887.

Nicolay, John G., and John Hay, eds. *Complete Works of Abraham Lincoln.* vol. 10. New York: Francis D. Tandy, 1905.

Opie, John N. *A Rebel Cavalryman.* Chicago: W.B. Conkey, 1899.

Pellet, Brevet-Major Elias P. *History of the 114th Regiment New York State Volunteers.* Norwich, NY: Telegraph & Chronicle Power Press Print, 1866.

Pond, George E. *The Shenandoah Valley in 1864.* New York: Jack Brussel, Pub., 1883.

Proceedings of the Senate and Assembly of the State of New York, of the Life and Services of Gen. Philip H. Sheridan, Held at the Capitol, April 9, 1889. Albany, NY: James B. Lyon, State Printer, 1890.

Rawling, C.J. *History of the First Regiment West Virginia Infantry.* Philadelphia: J.B. Lippincott, 1887.

Rhodes, Robert Hunt, ed. *All for the Union: The Civil War Diary and Letters of Elisha Hunt Rhodes.* New York: Vintage Books, 1985.

Runge, William H., ed. *Four Years in the Confederate Artillery: The Diary of Private Henry Robinson Berkeley*. Richmond: Virginia Historical Society, 1991.

Schmidt, Martin F., ed. *General George Crook: His Autobiography*. Norman: University of Oklahoma Press, 1946.

Sheridan, Philip H. *The Personal Memoirs of P.H. Sheridan*. New York: Charles L. Webster & Co., 1888.

Sprague, Homer B. *History of the 13th Infantry Regiment of Connecticut Volunteers During the Great Rebellion*. Hartford, CT: Case, Lockwood & Co., 1867.

Stevens, George T. *Three Years in the Sixth Corps: A Concise Narrative of Events in the Army of the Potomac, From 1861 to the Close of the Rebellion, April, 1865*. Albany, NY: S.R. Gray, Publisher, 1866.

Thacker, Victor L., ed. *French Harding: Civil War Memoirs*. Parsons, WV: McClain Printing, 2000.

Tieman, William F. *The 159th Regiment Infantry New York State Volunteers in the War of the Rebellion, 1862–1865*. Brooklyn, NY: self-published, 1891.

Walker, Aldace F. *The Vermont Brigade in the Shenandoah Valley, 1864*. Burlington, VT: The Free Press Association, 1869.

War Papers Read Before the Commandery of the State of Wisconsin, Military Order of the Loyal Legion of the United States. Milwaukee, WI: Burdick and Allen, 1914.

Wildes, Thomas F. *Record of the One Hundred and Sixteenth Regiment Ohio Infantry Volunteers in the War of the Rebellion*. Sandusky, OH: I.F. Mack & Bro., Printers, 1884.

Williams, Charles Richard, ed. *Diary and Letters of Rutherford Birchard Hayes: Nineteenth President of the United States.* Vol. 2. N.p.: The Ohio State Archaeological and Historical Society, 1922.

Worsham, John H. *One of Jackson's Foot Cavalry: His Experiences and What He Saw During the War 1861–1865*. New York: The Neal Publishing Co., 1912.

NEWSPAPERS

Baltimore American and Commercial Advertiser
Chicago Inter Ocean
The Evening Enterprise
The Evening Star
Harper's Weekly
National Tribune
News and Observer
New York Evening Post
The New York Herald
The New York Times
The New York Tribune
Spirit of Jefferson
Winchester News

Bibliography

Articles

Cox, William R. "Major-General Stephen D. Ramseur: His Life and Character." *Southern Historical Society Papers* 18 (1890): 217–60.

Fleischman, John. "The Object at Hand." *Smithsonian* (November 1996): 28–30.

Forsyth, George A. "Sheridan's Ride." *Harper's New Monthly Magazine*, July 1897, 165–81.

Harris, E. Ruffin. "Battle Near Cedar Creek, Va." *Confederate Veteran* 9, no. 9 (1901): 390.

McNeilly, Capt. J.S. "Battle of Cedar Creek." *Southern Historical Society Papers* 32 (1904): 223–39.

Noyalas, Jonathan A. "Jubal Early's 'Good Morning Salutation.'" *America's Civil War* 17, no. 5 (2004): 38–45.

Shewalter, Joseph D. "Observations on Sheridan's Ride." *Confederate Veteran* 23, no. 3 (1923): 88.

Suppiger, Joseph E. "Rienzi." *Lincoln Herald* 81, no. 3 (1979): 192–96.

A Surgeon in the Confederate Army. "The Battle of Cedar Creek." *Southern Historical Society Papers* 16 (1888): 443–47.

"A Visit to 'Sheridan's Ride.'" *Punchinello* 1, no. 3 (1870): 46.

Secondary Sources

Allen, T. Harrel. *Lee's Last Major General: Bryan Grimes of North Carolina*. Mason City, IA: Savas Publishing, 1999.

Barber, James G., ed. *Faces of Discord: The Civil War Era at the National Portrait Gallery*. New York: HarperCollins, 2006.

Beck, Brandon H., and Roger U. Delauter. *The Third Battle of Winchester*. Lynchburg, VA: H.E. Howard, 1997.

Beck, Brandon H., and Charles S. Grunder. *The Three Battles of Winchester: A History and Guided Tour.* Berryville, VA: The Civil War Foundation, 1997.

Blair, William. *Cities of the Dead: Contesting the Memory of the Civil War in the South, 1865–1914*. Chapel Hill: University of North Carolina Press, 2004.

Blight, David W. *Race and Reunion: The Civil War in American Memory*. Cambridge: Belknap Press, 2001.

Burr, Frank A., and Richard J. Hinton. *The Life of Gen. Philip H. Sheridan: Its Romance and Reality*. Providence, RI: J.A. and R.A. Reid Publishers, 1888.

Coffey, David. *Sheridan's Lieutenants: Phil Sheridan, His Generals, and the Final Year of the Civil War.* Lanham, MD: Rowman and Littlefield Publishers, Inc., 2005.

Coffin, Charles Carleton. *Freedom Triumphant: The Fourth Period of the War of the Rebellion, From September 1864, to Its Close*. New York: Harper and Brothers, 1890.

Cozzens, Peter. *Shenandoah 1862: Stonewall Jackson's Valley Campaign*. Chapel Hill: University of North Carolina Press, 2008.

DeLeon, T.C. *Crag's Nest: A Romance of the Days of Sheridan's Ride*. New York: G.W. Dillingham Co. Publishers, 1910.

Flood, Charles Bracelen. *1864: Lincoln at the Gates of History*. New York: Simon & Schuster, 2009.

Gallagher, Gary W. *Stephen D. Ramseur: Lee's Gallant General*. Chapel Hill: University of North Carolina Press, 1985.

———, ed. *The Shenandoah Valley Campaign of 1864*. Chapel Hill: University of North Carolina Press, 2006.

———, ed. *Struggle for the Shenandoah: Essays on the 1864 Valley Campaign*. Kent, OH: Kent State University Press, 1991.

Geier, Clarence, and Stephen R. Potter, eds. *Archaeological Perspectives on the American Civil War*. Gainesville: University Press of Florida, 2000.

Goss, Thomas J. *The War within the Union High Command: Politics and Generalship During the Civil War.* Lawrence: University Press of Kansas, 2003.

Hergesheimer, Joseph. *Sheridan: A Military Narrative*. Boston: Houghton Mifflin, 1931.

Higginson, Thomas Wentworth. *Young Folks Story of the United States*. Boston: Lee and Shepard, Publishers, 1887.

Holzer, Harold, ed. *Prang's Civil War Pictures: The Complete Battle Chromos of Louis Prang*. New York: Fordham University Press, 2001.

———. *The Union Image: Popular Prints of the Civil War North*. Chapel Hill: University of North Carolina Press, 2000.

Holzer, Harold, and Mark E. Neely Jr. *Mine Eyes Have Seen the Glory: The Civil War in Art*. New York: Orion, 1993.

Hoogenboom, Ari. *Rutherford B. Hayes: Warrior and President*. Lawrence: University Press of Kansas, 1995.

Leech, Margaret. *Reveille in Washington: 1860–1865*. New York: Harper and Brothers, 1941.

Lewis, Thomas A. *The Guns of Cedar Creek*. New York: Harper and Row, 1988.

Longacre, Edward G. *Lincoln's Cavalrymen: A History of the Mounted Forces of the Army of the Potomac*. Mechanicsburg, PA: Stackpole Books, 2000.

Mahr, Theodore C. *Early's Valley Campaign: The Battle of Cedar Creek: Showdown in the Shenandoah, October 1–30, 1864*. Lynchburg, VA: H.E. Howard, 1992.

McPherson, James J. *Tried by War: Abraham Lincoln as Commander-in-Chief*. New York: Penguin, 2008.

Noyalas, Jonathan A. *Plagued by War: Winchester, Virginia, During the Civil War*. Leesburg, VA: Gauley Mount Press, 2003.

Pope, Thomas E. *The Weary Boys: Col. J. Warren Keifer and the 110th Ohio Volunteer Infantry*. Kent, OH: Kent State University Press, 2002.

Sibler, Nina. *The Romance of Reunion: Northerners and the South, 1865–1900*. Chapel Hill: University of North Carolina Press, 1993.

Snell, Mark A. *From First to Last: The Life of Major General William B. Franklin*. New York: Fordham University Press, 2002.

Stackpole, Edward J. *Sheridan in the Shenandoah*. Harrisburg, PA: Stackpole Books, 1992.

Urwin, Gregory J.W. *Custer Victorious: The Civil War Battles of General George Armstrong Custer*. East Brunswick, NJ: Associated University Presses, 1983.

Wert, Jeffry D. *From Winchester to Cedar Creek: The Shenandoah Campaign of 1864.* Mechanicsburg, PA: Stackpole Books, 1997.

______. *The Sword of Lincoln: The Army of the Potomac*. New York: Simon and Schuster, 2005.

Williams, T. Harry. *Hayes of the Twenty-Third: The Civil War Volunteer Officer*. New York: Alfred A. Knopf, 1965.

About the Author

Jonathan A. Noyalas is assistant professor of history at Lord Fairfax Community College in Middletown, Virginia, and the author or editor of six books on Civil War–era history. Active in battlefield preservation, he serves on the board of directors of the Kernstown Battlefield Association and the committee on interpretation and education of the Shenandoah Valley Battlefields Foundation. Professor Noyalas is currently serving as the Civil War historian for the historic resource study at Cedar Creek and Belle Grove National Historical Park.

THE HISTORY PRESS

CIVIL WAR

SESQUICENTENNIAL SERIES

The History Press Civil War Sesquicentennial Series offers thoroughly researched, accessible accounts of important aspects of the war rarely covered outside the academic realm. Explore a range of topics from influential but lesser-known battles and campaigns to the local and regional impact of the war's figures—whether celebrated generals or common soldiers. Each book is crafted in a way that Civil War enthusiasts and casual readers alike will enjoy.

Books in this series from The History Press include:

The Chancellorsville Campaign
978.1.59629.594.0 * 6 x 9 * 160pp * $19.99

Defending South Carolina's Coast
978.1.59629.780.7 * 6 x 9 * 192pp * $21.99

Lee in the Lowcountry
978.1.59629.589.6 * 6 x 9 * 128pp * $19.99

The Union Is Dissolved!
978.1.59629.573.5 * 6 x 9 * 128pp * $19.99

The Civil War at Perryville
978.1.59629.672.5 * 6 x 9 * 192pp * $21.99